PRINCETON THEOLOGICAL MONOGRAPH SERIES

Dikran Y. Hadidian

General Editor

20

# THE PRESENT AND THE PAST
A Study of Anamnesis

# The
# Present
# and the
# Past

## A Study of Anamnesis

Richard J. Ginn

PICKWICK PUBLICATIONS
Allison Park, Pennsylvania

BV
4509.5
.G5
1989

Copyright © 1989 by Richard J. Ginn

Published by Pickwick Publications
4137 Timberlane Drive
Allison Park, PA 15101-2932

**Library of Congress Cataloging-in-Publication Data**

Ginn, Richard J.
    The present and the past : a study of anamnesis / by Richard
J. Ginn.
        p.    cm. -- (Princeton theological monograph series  :  20)
    Bibliography: p.
    ISBN 1-55635-004-X
    1. Recollection (Theology)  2. Recollection (Psychology)--
Biblical teaching.  3. History (Theology)--Biblical  teaching.
4. History  (theology)  5. History--Philosophy.   I. Title.   II.
Series.
    BV4509.5.05 1989
    231.7'6--dc20                                                        89-16056
                                                                              CIP

To the great British tradition of country parsons, their wives and families. In thankfulness for those whom God has given to me, and to whom I have been given. Especially for my wife Linda.

# CONTENTS

III.  An appraisal of the methodology and philosophy of the
        discipline of history

IV.  The Theology of History

# ACKNOWLEDGEMENTS

The author would like to thank Dr. Peter Toon for his guidance in supervising the thesis which was the basis for this book. The author is also indebted to Professor Kingsley Barrett of Durham for his encouragement and constructive criticism which has enabled this book to emerge; and to Professor Peter Ackroyd for his kindness in reading the proofs.

# CHAPTER ONE

# Patterns of Remembrance in Judaism to the time of Jesus Christ

## 1.1 Introduction

One of the most impressive aspects of Judaism is the extent to which it was preoccupied with tradition. Inherited traditions had a heavy influence on behavior: "Behold, I set before you this day a blessing and a curse; the blessing, if ye shall hearken unto the commandments of the Lord your God, which I command you this day: and the curse, if ye shall not hearken unto the commandments of the Lord your God, but turn aside out of the way which I command you this day, to go after other gods, which ye have not known". (Deut. 11:26-28). Judaism formed a network of teaching which aspired to cover the whole of life. Indeed, Judaism developed out of obedience to tradition in quest of a holy life: "Hear, O Israel: the Lord our God is one Lord: and thou shalt love the Lord thy God with all thine heart, and with all thy soul, and with all thy might". (Deut. 6:4-5).

Undergirding the whole of Judaism was the Old Testament. The Old Testament functioned as the basis of faith, as a reference manual, and as the court of appeal. It could be argued that Judaism emerged in "remembrance" of the Old Testament, for Judaism was inspired, conditioned, and regulated by the Old Testament.

A substantial problem in examining patterns in Judaism is the complicated way in which the celebration of specific occasions attracted a wider spectrum of remembrance. Consequently, it is very difficult to disentangle the original motives behind any festival. There is so much material available on the many festivals of Judaism, that it is necessary to focus on just two of the more significant strands in Judaism–the Sabbath and

the Passover. But first, it is important to note the way in which remembrance was consciously pursued in everyday life in physical signs
of the covenant.

## 1.2  Physical Signs of the Covenant

In Judaism there were four basic physical signs of the Covenant: Fringes, Phylacteries, Door-Post Symbols and Circumcision.

### Fringes
The Deuteronomic command: "Thou shalt make thee fringes upon the
four borders of thy vesture . . ." (Deut. 22:12) is amplified by the instructions in the book of Numbers: "And the Lord spake unto Moses,
saying, Speak unto the children of Israel and bid them that they make
them fringes in the borders of their garments throughout their generations . . . that ye may look upon it, and remember all the commandments of the Lord, and do them; and that ye go not about after your
own heart and your own eyes, after which ye used to go a whoring: that
ye may remember and do all my commandments, and be holy unto your
God". (Numbers 15:37-40). Thus the rather peripheral matter of a fringe
becomes something of great significance. There is no reference as to the
origin of 'fringes'. Fringes may have displaced older fashions of a different religious significance–but that is speculation. Equally, it would be
speculation to ponder any apotropaic significance of fringes. But the
possibility of an apotropaic significance to the fringe that was commonly recognized at the time of Jesus may be deduced from the rever-
ence that was paid to the 'fringe' of the clothing that Jesus wore (cf
Matthew 9:20; 14:36). Evidently the fringe was recognized as an em-
blem and almost as a talisman of sanctity.

Immense significance was invested in these fringes–to the extent that it
could be argued that no Jew was complete without them. Fringes were
intended to make Jews remember the commandments, so that they
would be "holy".

### Phylacteries
The commands concerning ornaments gave rise to the wearing of phylacteries: "Therefore shall ye lay up these words in your heart and in
your soul; and ye shall bind them for a sign upon your hand, and they

# INTRODUCTION

To the detached observer, the practice of Christianity displays a rather unusual feature in the believer's awareness of the past. Believers can have an approach to the Biblical narratives, particularly the Gospels, that is totally different from the approach that they would feel towards, for example, the biography of Julius Caesar. Furthermore, believers usually have a very different approach to the past described in the Bibli- cal narratives when compared with the approach of professed non- believers to the same material. Some explanation should be forthcom- ing to give account of the way in which people relate to the past, and particularly of the way in which believers relate to the past.

It is surprising how inadequate discussion of this area has been. Writers have tended to diverge into examining either the methodology of histor- ical study or the meaning of history, and there has been little explora- tion of the intermediate ground. The essential question is that of how people relate to the past. The fabric of the believer's relationship with the past must be explored. The relationship of people to the past is an inter-disciplinary problem involving philosophy, history and theology.

This study consists of five chapters. In the first two chapters, the pat- terns of remembrance in the Old and New Testament traditions are ex- amined, alongside the general understanding of history in the Bible. In the third chapter, an appraisal is made of the methodology and philoso- phy of the modern discipline of history. The limitations and the achievements of modern historical writing are thus brought into relief. In the fourth chapter, the theology of history is explored, and in the fi- nal chapter the implications of the distinctive character of anamnesis are drawn.

The bibliography is a comprehensive list of the books and articles that have been used in preparing this study. As far as I am aware, this is the only extensive bibliography in this precise line of study.

shall be for frontlets between your eyes" (Deut. 11:18). This verse is preceded by a threat to punish apostasy with drought and famine, and is followed by a promise that obedience will be rewarded with safe and enduring years in the promised land. The wearing of phylacteries is also directed in Deut. 6:8. However, in Exodus 13:9, 16 there are allusions to the practice of wearing phylacteries, linked respectively to the exodus from Egypt and the divine ownership of the firstborn. It may be that the wearing of phylacteries displaced pagan jewelry–but that, again, is speculation. But it is evident that the phylactery had a far greater significance than being a reminder of God's commands. Phylacteries were also considered to allude to God's work in redemption.

### Door-Post  Symbols
The symbols on door-posts functioned in the same way as personal phylacteries. They were instituted by Deuteronomic command (Deut. 6:9), but are without the extension of significance accorded to Phylacteries in Exodus. Once again, one can only speculate on any apotropaic significance in writing the words of the Lord upon door-posts, or whether this practice displaced some primitive recognition of "guardians of the threshhold". But in Isaiah 57:8 the charge against the apostates of Israel includes the challenge that pagan memorials have been set up behind "their doors and the posts". This was obviously a matter of considerable anxiety to the prophet as such a practice redefined a house and those who lived there as being dedicated to a different deity.

### Circumcision
Circumcision in Judaism is, technically, the removal of the male foreskin. Lev. 12:3 directs that: "in the eight day the flesh of his foreskin shall be circumcized." So, traditionally, the ceremony is performed when a boy is eight days old. Genesis 17:11 describes circumcision as a "token of a covenant" between God and Abraham, and the context links circumcision to the promised gift of the land of Canaan (v.8).

Circumcision had a particular religious significance for the Jews. Obviously, if circumcision was performed at eight days after birth, any previous linkage with puberty or marriage was lost, and circumcision became a sign of incorporation into the community of Israel. In Exodus 12:43-48, in the ordinance of the passover, circimcision is the qualification for joining in the passover. Thus, circumcision was a hallmark that entailed the recognition that one did belong to a distinctive community, and that one did live in the tradition that regarded the land of promise as one's own. Circumcision was more than a membership badge and functioned as a token of dedication.

## 1.3 Sabbath

In addition to the physical signs of the Covenant ran the regular weekly Sabbath. There are two strands of tradition which account for the origin of the Sabbath. Exodus 20:11 and Exodus 31:17 explain that the Sabbath represents the rest that God took on the seventh day from his work of creation. However, Deuteronomy 5:15 declares that the Sabbath is to be kept in order to remember the deliverance from Egypt. There is no clear evidence to show whether the Sabbath emerged in imitation of any pagan religious practice. But it needs to be appreciated that in both strands of Judaic tradition which account for the Sabbath, a common principle of remembrance is involved.

Exodus 20:8 says "Remember the sabbath day, to keep it holy." Exodus 31:13 instructs: "Verily ye shall keep my sabbaths: for it is a sign between me and you throughout your generations; that ye may know that I am the Lord which sanctify you." Both of these verses are followed by prohibitions of work on the Sabbath, and then these commands respectively conclude: "For in six days the Lord made heaven and earth, the sea and all that in them is, and rested the seventh day: wherefore the Lord blessed the sabbath day, and hallowed it" (Exodus 20:11). "Wherefore the children of Israel shall keep the sabbath, to observe the sabbath throughout their generations, for a perpetual covenant. It is a sign between me and the children of Israel for ever: for in six days the Lord made heaven and earth, and on the seventh day he rested, and was refreshed" (Exodus 31:16, 17). It is important here to note the sequence of thought. It is emphasized in both these versions of the fourth commandment that the Sabbath is observed so as to remember God's work in creation. Besides acting as a day when Jews were set free to worship, the day also put their own labors in perspective. The Jew was spurred to remember God by not allowing any distractions. The rest from work on the Sabbath was legitimized by being carried out in imitation of God.

In the Exodus commands, the Sabbath is a reminder to remember God:

"the seventh day is a sabbath of solemn rest, holy to the Lord" (Exodus 31:15). The Sabbath is not kept in remembrance of creation, rather the Sabbath is kept in order to remember God and his work. The parallel command in Deuteronomy (5:12-15) opens with the words: "Observe the sabbath day to keep it holy, as the Lord thy God commanded thee. Six days shalt thou labor, and do all thy work: but the seventh day is a sabbath unto the Lord thy God . . . ." There then follows a prohibition of work on the Sabbath and verse 15 concludes the commandment with the words: "And thou shalt remember that thou wast a servant in the land of Egypt, and the Lord thy God brought thee out thence by a mighty hand and by a stretched out arm: therefore the Lord thy God commanded thee to keep the sabbath day."

Once again, in Deuteronomy, the Sabbath functions as a reminder to remember God and his work. The divergence in the rationale of the Sabbath between the books of Deuteronomy and Exodus does not preclude the Sabbath from having a consistent overall purpose. Furthermore, the differences in the traditions illustrates the way that occasions of remembrance attract a wider spectrum of significance. In obedience to these commands the Sabbath emerged as a family day and as a day for worship and receiving instruction.

Sabbath observance generated a substantial literature in the Mishnah and Talmud which were formed well after the time of Jesus, but two particular verses from the book of Isaiah are traditionally taken to summarise the benefits of the sabbath: "If thou turn away thy foot from the sabbath, from doing thy pleasure on my holy day; and call the sabbath a delight, and the holy of the Lord honorable; and shalt honor it, not doing thine own ways, nor finding thine own pleasure, nor speaking thine own words; then shalt thou delight thyself in the Lord; and I will make thee to ride upon the high places of the earth; and I will feed thee with the heritage of Jacob thy father: for the mouth of the Lord hath spoken it" (Isaiah 58:13,14). These two verses underline the way that in Judaism the effects of the Sabbath fan out into the rest of life. Whilst the prohibition of work on the Sabbath affected the domestic routine of the whole week, the Sabbath as a pattern of remembrance aspired to produce an on-going devotional life that dominated a Jew's whole behavior.

## 1.4 Passover

Whilst the Sabbath has some problems attaching to its origin, the Passover presents an even more complicated picture. Exodus 12:1-20 presents a tangle of interwoven traditions which has prompted many attempts to trace the possible derivation of the extant text. The Passover, the Feast of Unleavened Bread, and the Redemption of the firstborn are all important elements in this passage.

The Passover developed from a family feast to a centralized pilgrimage (Deut. 16:1-8). The lively enthusiasm of the festival in the time of Jesus is amply attested in the Gospels. The Passover traditionally functioned as a celebration of divine deliverance and God-given liberty. Once again, there is an active principle of remembrance at work – the Passover acted as a reminder to remember God and his work: "And this day shall be unto you for a memorial, and ye shall keep it a feast to the Lord: throughout your generations ye shall keep it a feast by an ordinance for ever". (Exodus 12:14). "And Moses said unto the people, Remember this day, in which ye came out from Egypt, out of the house of bondage; for by strength of hand the Lord brought you out from this place . . . " (Exodus 13:3).

Of particular interest for this study is the role of the Passover Lamb and the way that it came to be understood. After the destruction of the Temple in A.D. 70, the Passover sacrifices came to an end, and much of the material interpreting the Passover may be plausibly suggested to have been lost or re-worked so that only vestiges remain of the older patterns of remembrance in later Judaism.

De Vaux summarizes modern speculation on the origins of the use of a Lamb at Passover: "It is the kind of sacrifice which nomads or semi-nomads offer, and no other sacrifice in all Israelite ritual is more like the sacrifices of the ancient Arabs: there is no priest, no altar, and the use of the blood is most important. The Passover was the spring-time sacrifice of a young animal in order to secure fecundity and prosperity for the flock. The purpose of putting blood upon the stiles of the door (originally, on the tent poles) was to drive away evil powers . . ."[1] If this is a true account of the derivation of the Passover sacrifice, it is noteworthy that, as with the Passover Lamb, there is no basic intention of expiation or atonement. Thus, in Exodus 12:1-14, there is no mention of any wish to propitiate the Lord, only a desire to secure his protection. Specifically there is the implication of the passover securing protection for the first-born of Israel. It was only the first-born who are recorded to have died, and because of the blood of the lambs, only the first-born of Egypt died. A sacrificial lamb is also referred to in connection with the Redemption of the Firstborn (Exodus 13:11-16). And the redemption of the first-born is also linked to the final plague and the Exodus–again a reminder to remember: "And it shall be for a sign upon thine hand and for frontlets between thine eyes: for by strength of hand the Lord brought us forth out of Egypt" (Exodud 13:16). So, again, two apparently independent practices have interacted and spilled over into each other within the traditions of the Exodus.

Also aggregated within the Exodus traditions was the feast of unleavened bread. Exodus 12:15-20 and 13:6-10 relate the ordinance. Within the context of the narrative, the institution of the feast of unleavened bread is specifically related to the exigencies of the Exodus. It may be that the feast of unleavened bread was a tradition that was adopted after arrival in Canaan, where it has been suggested that the feast marked the first week of harvest. In this case the link is reinforced between the Exodus and the Promised Land. Exodus 12:19 emphasizes that abstaining from the unleavened food for the week was essential to remaining within the congregation of Israel. And Exodus 13:9 held that keeping the feast "shall be for a sign unto thee upon thine hand, and for a memorial between thine eyes, that the law of the Lord may be in thy mouth . . . "

## 1.5 The Akedah

One pattern of exegesis which succeeded in bringing together the Passover and the Redemption of the Firstborn, and which probably developed in the inter-testamental period, focused on the "Akedah"–the binding of Isaac, Abraham's first-born son. As within the Pentateuch occasions of remembrance tended to osmose and broaden into the general run of tradition, so within the surviving indications of the devotional awareness of first century Judaism this tendency developed so that a variety of exegesis clustered around the Akedah. In the Book of Jubilees (18:18-19) it is said that after the incident of the Akedah, Abraham fixed an annual seven-day festival as a memorial of the seven days he spent journeying to the land of Moriah and returning from it in peace. Further, in the Book of Jubilees the Akedah has the same date as Passover, and there is the implication that Passover is the anniversary of Isaac's sacrifice. It has also been deduced that within the drama of the Akedah there is a divine rejection of the practice of sacrificing human first-born. And a ram is substituted for Isaac. The Passover therefore not only celebrates the liberation from bondage, but also celebrates the deliverance from paganism. Further, there is evidence from the Palestinian Targums arising from the association of Genesis 22 with Isaiah 53 that for the Palestinian Jew of the first century, the sacrifice of Isaac had come to be regarded as a self-offering.

This pattern of thinking developed so that the Akedah, although ritually incomplete because Isaac was not killed, yet came to be considered to be a true sacrifice and Israel's main title to forgiveness and redemption. The slaughter of the Passover lambs and the Temple tradition of sacrificial worship was to remind God of Isaac's self-sacrifice and to invoke his merits. In the *Mekilta of Rabbi Ishmael* this line of thought was acknowledged with an haggadic comment on the Institution of the Passover (Exodus 12:13): the clause "And when I see the blood" is interpreted to mean: "I see the blood of the sacrifice of Isaac."[2]

It is important to note that the possibility of understanding the Akedah in the way that has been outlined above was countenanced, and further illustrates the way that the celebration of specific occasions attracted a far wider spectrum of remembrance. The haggadah of the Akedah drew together loosely connected elements in the Passover narrative and explicated the sacrifice of the Passover lamb. However, if the Akedah is embraced as anything more than a possible explanation of the Passover, then the theology of remembrance that has emerged so far in this study is set aside. In the haggadah of the Akedah the purpose of the slaughter of the Passover Lamb was to remind God of Isaac's perfect act of oblation and to invoke his merits. Maybe this reflected a desire to understand the Passover Lamb as an expiatory sacrifice. Certainly Vermes regards the theology of Akedah as an important preparation of the groundwork of understanding for the coming of Christianity. Vermes claims that in Palestine: "The Akedah was considered a sacrifice of Redemption, the source of pardon, salvation and eternal life, through the merits of Abraham who loved God so greatly as to offer Him his only son, but principally through the merits of Isaac, who offered his life voluntarily to his Creator."[3] Thus the Passover Lamb is suggested to recall the Akedah and to prefigure the Atonement.

The haggadah of the Akedah represents the conflation of two aspects of the cultus of Judaism. One aspect is the traditions by which people were reminded to live in remembrance of their God. The other aspect which is outside the focus of this study is the ongoing ritual, including sacrifice, in which people presented themselves before God. In this conflation there is also a confusion that is absent from the structure of the Biblical narratives. Whilst the Akedah illuminates the popular appreciation of the Passover and the Redemption of the First-born, the Akedah generates a doctrinal tangle if it is viewed as anything more than an interpretative hypothesis.

## 1.6 Remembrance in Cultic Memorials

At this point it is useful to review the patterns of remembrance surveyed so far. All alike have functioned primarily as reminders to remember God and his work. But as they derive from an era in which theology was expressed, at least in part, by describing the work of God, it proved to be impossible to maintain a discrete reference in remembrance. Thus, just as it is impossible to pursue one of the attributes of God in isolation from all the rest, so also it was impossible to focus on the remembrance of one revelatory occasion to the exclusion of all others. Futhermore, remembrance was active, not passive; and therefore remembrance was confessional. That is to say that remembrance was a recognizable pattern of activity that showed what was believed. One verse that summarizes the Judaic theology of remembrance is Isaiah 46:9: " Remember the former things of old: for I am God, and there is none else; I am God, and there is none like me".

Remembrance affirmed belief in God and also belief in the presence of God. Much discussion has taken place around the process of remembrance in the cult. The opinion has gathered that to remember within the cult was to actualize the past. Noth and Childs are but two of the many scholars who have been committed to this view; "Israel celebrated in her seasonal festivals the great redemptive acts of the past both to renew the tradition and to participate in its power."[4] But the suggestion is implausible in the long-term because of its complexity. Remembrance affirmed belief in the presence and the power of God, not in the presence of the past. As one would expect, this is amply borne out in the psalter. Time and again the psalter returns to the theme of the presence and the power of God and of the experience of being in his presence.

## 1.7 The Understanding of Time in Judaism

The distinctive relationship in Judaism between the present and the past indicates that the Jews had a distinctive understanding of history. Usually, it has been the practice of people writing about the Jewish understanding of history to start by comparing the Jewish and Greek notions of time. The evidence for the alleged differences can be put into three groups. Firstly, it has been suggested that as the Hebrew verb includes only "perfectum" and "imperfectum" and has no future tense, the Jews did not possess the linguistic instruments to think historically. Secondly, it has been maintained that as the Jews had no specific word for "time", they were unable to formulate the absract notion of chronological succession. Thirdly, some scholars[5] have maintained that the Greeks conceived of time as a cycle, whereas the Jews conceived of time as a progression "ad finitum" or "ad infinitum", so that time was viewed as a line by the Jews and a circle by the Greeks. Cullman particularly has invested heavily in this last point,[6] but Barr has made an extensive study which effectively dismantled this whole speculative structure.[7]

The first point above is perhaps the strangest. The absence of a Hebrew future tense certainly did not prevent the Jews from developing a proper historical sense, and therefore a historiography, it is self-evident that the formulation of Jewish historical writing was on the broadest page, framed by the sense of being between the beginning and the end, and the biblical narratives would have been impossible to compile without an awareness of chronological succession. The second point also can be dealt with by an appeal to evidence. Biblical Hebrew does have words for time and eternity. But the books of the Bible (with the exception of Ecclesiastes) do not contain extended meditations about time such as are found in the writings of Greek poets and philosophers. Whilst certain theories about time are indeed to be found in Plato and not in the Bible, it overstretches the evidence to say that Hebrew words as such imply a different conception of time. On the third point it suffices to note that the demarcation between Greek and Hebrew thought is not clearcut. The expectation of an annual cycle of religious festivities was common to both. And, like the writers of I Kings and II Kings, Thucydides and Herodotus were well aware that the same things did not repeat themselves from year to year. Certainly, it has been demonstrated that there is no standardized idea of time in the extant writings of Ancient Greece,[8] so it is impossible to compare Biblical thought with Greek thought because there is no standard opinion on this subject in Greek literature. Altogether, it appears that the effort to understand the character of history in the Bible by comparing biblical thought with an artificially homogenized Greek thought has been a false trail.

## 1.8 The Distinctive Features of the Jewish Understanding of History

From any plain reading of canonical scripture, a huge variety of factors is reflected in the writing and use of narrative. Political, ethnic, economic and devotional factors, along with many others, interplay so as to produce a kaleidoscope of great subtlety that despite all its editing has not been homogenized. The Old Testament has come down to us as a whole, and yet whilst it is differentiated into various groups of books within the Jewish tradition, there is nevertheless an overall understanding of history that may be deduced.

Firstly, there is the continuity of narrative from the creation to about 400 BC. Within the literature of the ancient world, the Biblical sequence of narrative was a unique achievement. The building blocks of the original independent historical works which were shaped to more or less fit together gradually became subsumed under the schema of an historical continuum. This sense of continuity in history is quite remarkable. From time to time it has been fashionable to disparage Ancient Israel in contrast with the more intellectually refined Athens or Rome. There seems to be a lurking suspicion of the "primitive" character of Jewish thought, almost to the extent of regarding it as a mildly domesticated nomadism. And yet the Jews were capable of amassing very substantial historical traditions.

Secondly, another aspect of the Jewish understanding of history was that reliability was not a criterion in choosing data for inclusion in history. There is no impulse for authenticating traditional material. There was no felt need for example, that is discernible from surviving material, to obtain evidence for the manner of the death of Enoch or for the age of Methuselah. Tradition carried its own authority as it became sublimated as written narrative. This illustrates the way that history was confessional for the Jews. They selected and recited their history to show what they believed.

Thirdly, remembering the past was a religious duty. This made the role of history even more important as the record of the years between the Exodus and the present. The historians not only recorded the impression of the judges and kings but also evaluated the national and regal fidelity to the sovereignty of God. This links up with a remark by Childs that Israel's memory serves: "a far more important role than merely providing illustrations from the past. It serves in making Israel noetically aware of a history which is ontologically a unity."[9] The recital of the acts of God in the past therefore acts as a statement of belief about God in the present. There was one history because there is one God. There was a continuous history because God has always been God (cf. Psalm 90:1,2).

Finally, there was a distinction between the Hebrew historians and the prophets. The historians set the context for Elijah and Elishah, but there is the clear impression that the historian subordinates himself to the prophet and derives his values from the prophets. At worst the historians may have been political scribes, determined to sustain a Davidic kingdom. But at best they played Baruch to God's Jeremiahs and so underlined the religious character of history in Hebrew thought. Old Testament history was a medium for expressing divine truth. Perhaps this may explain why some books never came to be preserved, for example, the Book of Jashar (Joshua 10:13), the Acts of Solomon (I Kings 11:41).

## 1.9 Conclusion

Remembrance bridged past and present. The intricate pattern of reminders to remember continually confronted the pious Jew and challenged him to hold his God in memory. Remembrance emerges as a pattern of historical understanding. Remembrance controlled the content of history, and the use of history. Remembrance in Judaism was a pattern of life which transformed chronicle into confession. The distinctive approach to history in the Old Testament was expressed in, and reinforced by, the labor of amassing a comprehensive corpus of tradition.

In remembrance, traditions were employed in which historical information was subordinated to the purposes of worship and adoration. Information about the past was recalled within the context of the enduring purposes of God. And this recall combined with the physical signs of the covenant to issue in a present encounter with God. To hold God in memory meant to live in his presence.

# NOTES

1. R. de Vaux, **Ancient Israel: Its Life and Institutions**, (London, 1974): 489.
2. Ed. J. Z. Lauterbach, **Mekilta de-Rabbi Ishmael**, (Philadelphia, 1976): Vol. I, 57.
3. Vermes, **Scripture and Tradition in Judaism**, (Leiden, 1973): 219.
4. Childs, **Memory and Tradition in Israel**, (London, 1962): 75.
5. E.g. J. Baillie (in **The Belief in Progress**) and Richardson (in **History, Sacred and Profane**).
6. Cullmann, **Christ and Time**, (London, 1967).
7. Barr, **Biblical Words for Time**, (London, 1969).
8. Momigliano, "Time in Ancient Historiography" in Beiheft 6 of **History and Theory**, (Connecticut, 1966).
9. Childs, **Memory and Tradition in Israel**, (London, 1962): 52.

# CHAPTER TWO

# Anamnesis in the New Testament

## 2.1 Textual Considerations

The starting point for the study of remembrance in the New Testament
has to be the study of the use of the word *anamnesis*. This word is
found in four verses in the New Testament–Luke 22:19; 1 Corinthians
11:24,25; and Hebrews 10:3. The text of Luke 22:19 has been the subject of dispute because some of the words, including *anamnesis*, are
omitted in Codex Bezae and in some later manuscripts. However, the
state of the argument on this matter has been reviewed by Howard Marshall,[1] and he concludes: "The external evidence for the longer text is
overwhelming. The weakness of the argument lies in  accounting for
the origin of the shorter text . . . , but this may be due simply to some
scribal idiosyncrasy. On balance the longer text is to be preferred."

## 2.2 Lexical Considerations

The word *anamnesis* was taken up into the Greek New Testament having already been used in the Septuagint. It is possible to try to build a
picture of a distinctive shade of meaning of the word in its use in the
LXX[2] and to build an elaborate hypothesis as to the distinction between
*anamnesis* and the more usual word for remembrance/memorial in the
LXX - the word *mnemosunon*. *Mnemosunon* is used over forty times
in the canonical sections of the LXX. The variety of context includes
the sense of a memorial written in a book (Exodus 17:14); a memorial
of blowing of trumpets (Leviticus 23:24); a memorial warning that
only priests should approach the altar (Numbers 16:40); the memorial
stones at the crossing of the Jordan (Joshua 4:7); the memorial of a
good reputation (Psalm 111:6) and even an impious offering of frankin-
cense (Isaiah 66:3). It is not possible to deduce any special meaning for

*mnemosunon* beyond the general sense of remembrance/memorial used as qualified by its context. It is only used in six places to describe an offering made in course of regular divine sacrificial worship. The first three are Leviticus 2:2,9,16 where *mnemosunon* is the word for the fraction of a sacrificial offering that is actually burnt. The second three are Numbers 5:15,18,26. Again *mnemosunon* describes the fraction of a sacrifical offering that is burnt, as well as the whole of the offering from which it is drawn, but this time the context is of a man taking his wife to the priest under suspicion of infidelity. Perhaps the word *mnemosunon* had had too many uses to be readily useful in the narratives of the Last Supper. The three times that the word is used in the New Testament do not settle the matter. Matthew 26:13 and Mark 14:9 are parallel verses referring to the memorial of the woman who poured ointment over Jesus. In Acts 10:4 the angel declares that the alms of Cornelius are "gone up for a memorial before God". Nothing definitive may be deduced from the use of *mnemosunon* in the Greek Bible, and its use carries little implication for the significance of the word *anamnesis*.

The word *anamnesis* is used only twice in the LXX text of the canonical books: In Leviticus 24:7 the loaves of the shew bread are said to be "for a remembrance, set forth before the Lord". In Numbers 10:10, at the end of a short section of instructions about making two silver trumpets and when to use them, the Israelites were told: "and in the days of your gladness, and in your feasts, and in your new moons, you shall sound with the trumpets at your whole burnt offerings, and at the sacrifices of your peace offerings; and there shall be a remembrance for you before your God . . . ." Nothing determinative may be derived from such a paucity of material, except to note that the word *anamnesis* had no special meaning for the compilers of the LXX, as it is qualified both times with the rider attached that the remembrance was before the Lord God. So the word itself does not inherently contain any specific direction of remembrance, whether before man or before God, unless some qualification is given. This is born out in the titles of the two Psalms where the word *anamnesis* appears. Psalm 37 in the LXX carries the title "A Psalm of David for remembrance concerning the sabbath", and the word *anamnesis* would be left in suspense if it were not for the first word of the Psalm, addressing it clearly to the Lord. The title of Psalm 69 in the LXX is more specific: "To the end, by David for remembrance, that the Lord may save me." The only other point at which the word *anamnesis* is used in the LXX, at Wisdom 16:6, there is a warning to hold a token of salvation for remembrance of the command of the Law, and here remembrance is clearly directed at the people. From this short review it is clear that, like *mnemosunon*, *anamnesis* has no special meaning beyond a general sense of remembrance/memorial and, when used, is qualified to give it direction either before God or before man. It cannot be assumed or asserted that *anamnesis* is a technical term with a precise meaning that can be unfolded by lexical research.

But still one may be left with the suspicion that *anamnesis* is used as a special term in the Institution Narrative because it has a special context. A helpful line of approach is to examine the use of *anamnesis* and its synonym *hupomnesis* where they occur outside the institution narratives. In 2 Peter 1:13 and 2 Peter 3:1 *hupomnesei* appears linked respectively to the words *humas* and *humon*. There is nothing particularly remarkable about *hupomnesis* in 2 Timothy 1:5 except that it avoids the repetition of the root *MNE* at the start of a third word, *mneian* having occurred in verse 3 and *memnemenos* in verse 4. However, in Hebrews 10:3 the use of *anamnesis* is obviously dictated by a stylistic pursuit of alliteration. It may, therefore, be plausible to suggest that the usage of *anamnesis* and *hupomnesis* is controlled by other than lexical considerations, for example a desire for alliteration or for euphony. *Eis ten emon anamnesin* would sound far better in a liturgical context than *eis to emon mnemosunon*. Euphony is a far more likely determinative influence on a clause that is significant in oral divine worship than lexical pedigree could ever be. Even if the word *anamnesis* is used in a special context, it does not necessarily have to have a specialized technical meaning.

By the time the anamnesis clause was recorded it was already a tradition and had, therefore, already been shaped by usage. The general meaning of *anamnesis* may therefore be taken as being "remembrance" with no particular shade of meaning other than that which is conferred in the context of its use.

## 2.3 The Passover and the Last Supper

The understanding of the anamnesis clause is conditioned by many factors. Once a textual and lexical basis is established, the clause then must have its meaning shaped by its context. There has been substantial controversy on the exact nature of the Last Supper. It is reasonable to accept that in character the meal had a general Passover atmosphere. But whether the Synoptic date of the meal at the official Passover hour is correct, or whether the Johannine dating before the official Passover is correct, or whether it is possible that the use of two different calendars makes them both correct, cannot be decided, and there is no scholarly consensus on the matter. In the Synoptic account of the Last Supper, Jesus identifies himself with the bread and wine. By contrast, in the Fourth Gospel, Jesus is identified from the start as the "Lamb of God" (John 1:29,36). The omission of the Institution Narrative from the Fourth Gospel may have been a deliberate decision to avoid confusion with the motif of Jesus being the "Lamb of God"–a factor which finds its fullest expression when Jesus dies at the time of the slaughter of the Passover Lambs (John 19:36/Exod 12:46). It is not the purpose of this study to attempt to resolve either the problem of the exact nature of the Last Supper, which has attracted an enormous literature, or the problem of the timing of the passion. But, having noted the existence of these problems it is necessary that any understanding of "remembrance" has to do justice to both the Synoptic and the Johannine traditions.

## 2.4 Considerations of Interpretation

The context of the institution of the Lord's Supper is crucial for the understanding of the anamnesis clause. Jeremias has been adamant that the Last Supper was a Passover meal, and yet even he has suggested a considerable variation in the interpretation of this clause. Jeremias has rejected the traditional translation of the clause "do this in remembrance of me" in the sense: "Do this so that you will remember me", and has declared that the clause means: Do this "that remembrance should be made of me."[3] Jeremias goes on to try to show that this clause in the Institution Narrative is a prayer for God's remembrance of Jesus. Jeremias postulates that the anamnesis clause is a prayer that God should remember the Messiah by bringing about His Kingdom in the parousia. If the Passover context is dominant at the Last Supper then the association would conspire to make the remembrance which Jesus commanded comparable to the remembrance inherent in Passover. In the Passover, the participant in the first place looked back and remembered and was reminded of the power of God and of his presence. In the Eucharist, the Christian would also look back and remember and be reminded. The very economy of the traditional words of Jesus precludes any ambiguity.

Gore was aware of the possibility of this line of interpretation at the turn of the century and felt that this approach would be plausible but for the fact that it was not so understood by the Church in the early centuries. The internal evidence of the early anaphoras contradicts this hypothesis. Thus, for example, in the *Apostolic Tradition of Hippolytus* (4:11) we read: "remembering therefore his death and resurrection, we offer . . . "; in the anaphora of Basil of Caesarea we read after the anamnesis: "We also, remembering his holy sufferings, and his resurrection from the dead, and his return to heaven . . ." There is the clear implication that in the early Church the words of institution meant "This do to remember me".

The plain meaning of remembrance in the anamnesis clause is given clear direction by the context, that the *disciples* should have Jesus in remembrance.

A further source of confusion in the appreciation of *anamnesis* can come from taking into consideration some of the writings of Philo. At three points in his works[4] Philo had a discussion of the meaning of anamnesis. For him it meant recollection after forgetfulness and was quite subordinate to a continuous power of recall in memory (*mnemes*). It should be noted that within his work, Philo turns anamnesis into a technical term that is irrelevant to this study.

Having clarified the general meaning of the anamnesis clause - "do this in remembrance of me", one other factor should be mentioned in its interpretation. Remembrance in the Passover did not exclusively refer to things of the past, but could also refer to something future. Remembrance at the Passover not only looked back to past deliverance, but also looked forward to future deliverance. The Passover looked both to the Exodus and to the Coming of the Messiah. Similarly the Lord's Supper is regarded by Paul as looking to both the Crucifixion and the Parousia (1 Corinthians 11:26).

## 2.5 The Akedah discounted as an Interpretation of the Passion

There has been a growing interest in the haggadah of the Akedah–the binding of the only son of Abraham. This area of investigation has taken on the aura of the emergence of the discovery of a missing link between the Old and the New Testaments. Particularly, the Akedah is seen to assist in explaining the sufferings of the Messiah. Whilst the Passover Lamb with which Jesus appeared to identify himself, was not in itself an expiatory sacrifice, yet Isaac's self-offering was in the haggadah an expiatory sacrifice that was remembered in the Passover, and which could be argued apologetically to have been fulfilled and perfected in the sacrifice of the new Isaac–the only son of God. But the paucity of sources about the Akedah (especially the silence of the known Dead Sea Scrolls on this subject) makes it an insecure plank in any argument. The only clearcut allusion to the Akedah in the New Testament is to be found in Romans 8:32, reproducing words from Genesis 22:16; but this is only an allusion, not even a direct reference.

In any case, even if there had been discussion of the haggadah of the Akedah amongst the disciples of Jesus, it would have been surprising if this discussion had gone unchecked, since Jesus was impatient with anything less than "the law and the prophets". Whilst there may have been a diffused understanding of the Akedah in Palestine in the time of Christ of which he may have been tempted to take advantage, it would be arguable equally that this was one of the many erroneous religious tendencies against which Jesus struggled. Thus just as it may be argued from silence that the Palestinian view of the Akedah colored Jesus' self-understanding and formed part of the unrecorded early Christian apologetic, so also it may be argued from silence that the second temptation in Matthew 4:6 where Jesus was tempted with words based on Psalm 91:11, 12, reflected the temptation to model himself as the new Isaac. For the quotation: "He shall give his angels charge concerning thee: and on their hands shall they bear thee up . . . " have an uncanny echo to the words of the Palestinian Targum that come after the seminal promise to Abraham: "And the angels on high took Izhak and brought him into the school of Shem the Great; and he was there three years."[5] It is never  said that angels took charge of Jesus, but rather that they ministered to him. Clearly arguments from silence cannot be determinative in establishing haggadah as dogma, and the Akedah as an interpretation of the Passion begins to look unlikely.

Another defect in this haggadah was that by the Akedah the obedience of sacrifice was translated into a way of securing the merit of Isaac. But the proper scriptural reason that sacrifices were considered to be valid and efficacious was because they were carried out in response to the command of God. Perhaps the strongest obstacle to accepting the haggadah of the Akedah is the simple fact that St Paul does not present Jesus as the new Isaac but as the new Adam. If there had been any apologetic advantage in using the Akedah to persuade people of the truth of Christianity, we may be fairly confident that Paul would have both known about it and used it. If the Akedah did have any appeal to a Jewish audience, that may be why the early Christian writers who did allude to the Akedah were mainly from Alexandria with its significant Jewish population. Clement, Origin and Cyril all mentioned Isaac as a type or picture of Christ's sacrifice, but only a handful of times between them.[6] Finally, it is worth mentioning the thought that maybe why Jesus was without honor in his own country and why he was rejected as the Messiah was because he refused to be the new Isaac. It is not therefore clear that the theology of the Akedah makes any definitive contribution to the understanding of the Passover.

## 2.6 Last Supper and Lord's Supper

Institution Narratives are to be found in Matthew 26:26-29; Mark 14:22-25; Luke 22:15-20; and 1 Corinthians 11:23-26. The most significant of the variations between the sources is that 1 Corinthians and Luke contain a command to repeat the observance, while Mark and Matthew do not. There appears to be general agreement that the whole sequence of Supper, Crucifixion, and Resurrection took place against the background of Passover. However, some of the issues in the relationship between the Last Supper and the Lord's Supper of the Christian Church have to be reviewed. This again has been a considerable area of debate. Drawing the threads together, it is broadly considered that if the Last Supper had been instituted to be a proper Passover Supper, then the Eucharist would have been developed into an annual observance. Furthermore, it can be argued that Mark's account of the Last Supper deliberately identifies the rite instituted by Jesus Christ with the liturgical eucharist as celebrated during the years 65-70 in the Gentile-Christian Church of Rome. This can be taken to explain the omission of the anamnesis clause in Mark on the basis that a command to repeat was unnecessary when repetition was an established practice anyway. Dix found a substantial contrast between Mark and St. Paul.[7] Dix suggested that St Paul's account in 1 Corinthians 11 is more concerned with the history of the Last Supper than with its interpretation. In Dix's estimation, St Paul regarded the death of Christ as the Passover (cf 1 Corinthians 5:7) rather than regarding the Last Supper as the Passover. If this is the case, then Paul was at one with St. John. So it could be suggested that the compiler of St Matthew's gospel omitted the anamnesis clause in imitation of St Mark's gospel, whilst the compiler of the third gospel incorporated this clause out of deference to his reputed mentor St Paul.

It is probably as important to take into account a wide spectrum of views on this matter as it is important not to come to any definite conclusion. If a definite conclusion was reached about the nature of the Last Supper and the link between the death of Jesus and the Passover, this would entail a precise reference in any act of eucharistic remembrance in the Church. But the Eucharist took the place of all the Jewish sacrifices and feasts, and not just the place of the Passover and Unleavened Bread. It therefore may be more appropriate to base the exegesis of the anamnesis clause on a far wider appreciation than a mere definition. It has already been shown that a lexical analysis is not an adequate method. Equally, it is probably inadequate to regard the anamnesis clause as being exhaustively defined by a precise historical referent.

The Passover is certainly the background for the Last Supper, but no equation can be drawn between the two. The anamnesis clause says "Do this in remembrance of me", not "Do this in remembrance of my death", and therefore is perhaps not susceptible of any complete analysis. The whole sequence of the Last Supper, the Crucifixion, and the Resurrection, took place against the background of Passover, thus the Easter events are held closely together and were on the whole bound to be interpreted from the first in terms of the Passover. So as the anamnesis clause has a wider reference than the Crucifixion, then it is only proper that anamnesis be understood in terms of the whole background of remembrance as practiced in Judaism.

## 2.7  Remembrance transfused from Judaism into Christianity

If there was no continuity between remembrance in Judaism and the meaning of the anamnesis clause, then it could be argued that this clause would have been unintelligible to the apostles. Knight has explored the way that tradition operated in Judaism. Knight found that: "Tradition constitutes the pre-understanding and pre-condition for revelation . . . Tradition delivers the framework - intellectual, historical, religious, hermeneutical - needed for a new event or word to be meaningful."[8] It follows, therefore, that as remembrance was integrated into Christianity, so the main characteristics which remembrance had exhibited in Judaism were also transfused into Christianity. Thus remembrance in Christianity could not be a straightforward "remembering", rather remembrance had confessional implications and the anamnesis of Jesus Christ could not be exhaustively defined in terms of his death. Again, remembrance attracted a wider spectrum of reference than a precise historical event, and the anaphoras declared that the faithful remembered a great chain of events in the work of Jesus Christ. The disciples found their allegiance to God channelled through their Master, so that in remembering him, they encountered God. Furthermore, the recital of God's activity in and through Jesus Christ became a further part of their description of God.

The exhortation "do this in remembrance of me" carries with it a great many claims, particularly claims as to some sort of pre-eminence on the part of Jesus Christ. It is not the purpose of this study to evaluate the christological import of Jesus Christ. Instead some examination will be made of the implications of "remembrance" for the understanding of history.

## 2.8  Remembrance and the New Testament Understanding of History

There is a theme in the Old Testament of the transitory nature of the earth (e.g. Psalm 102:25-27, Isaiah 40:6-8, 51:6). God is distinguished from the creation and is set over against created things. The saying of Jesus that "Heaven and earth will pass away, but my words will not pass away" (Mark 13:31) fit into this general tradition of understanding. Many scholars feel that this saying has to do with the teaching of Jesus as a whole, and that Jesus claimed an eternal validity for His teaching--valid not only in the present age, but also for the age to come. The Rabbis debated whether the sacred Law would continue in full force in the world to come. So this saying of Jesus in effect puts his teaching on a higher level of authority than the Law. The general thrust of the New Testament values obedience to Jesus Christ, but does not appear to lay any great value on world affairs. Value is attached, in the Pauline epistles and elsewhere, to people honestly earning a living. But otherwise, the only general expectation about the world in the New Testament is that the world is transient (2 Peter 3:10). The works of love are valued, but not the affairs of the world.

At first sight the New Testament may be thought to be rather innocent about history--until measure is taken of the supremacy accorded to Jesus Christ. As St. Paul wrote: "God highly exalted him, and gave unto him the name which is above every name; that in the name of Jesus every knee should bow . . ." (Philippians 2:9ff). If Jesus Christ occupies such an exalted position, even eschatologically, then there is no room for anyone or anything else to occupy any final position of authority.

International politics as a set of competing political hierarchies founded on fixed geographical land areas has its role severely questioned by the status of the exalted Lord. Paul wrote that the governing authorities of this earth were "ordained of God" (Romans 13:1). Preiss insisted that "in spite of the ambivalence of the state the Christian must serve it in the light of justice. All these powers are in principle subject not only to God but to Christ. They are not vaguely subordinated to the far-off direction of a general providence . . . but they are responsible before Christ. States and all historic dignities belong to the cosmic *regnum Christi*. As for all the powers which secular history speaks of as collective powers and movements and 'isms', . . . the Bible personifies them to show that these powers are responsible, that they are indeed collective responsibilities, but also to emphasize that men are no more than their agents and their victims. Above all, the Bible proclaims that none of these realities is final."[9]

One of the problems in formulating theology's approach to history is to work out the nature of the reality of institutions invested with corporate identities. It is not even certain how to state this problem clearly.

World affairs are no longer solely the product of the interplay of sovereign nation-states, let alone the outcome of rival empires. For example, the modern international commercial corporation is of colossal import in world affairs. Corporate identity is not the exclusive possession of states. Any theological assessment of the reality of corporate identity has to take account of international corporations, and of national institutions and local concerns as well.

In the Old Testament, considerable weight is attached to national identities. Many chapters are given to the judgment of the nations, and the nations are addressed as individuals. However, it could be argued that the names of the nations are symbols for national patterns of life. In addition, it could be argued that all institutions which claim, or are given, a corporate identity are using their titles as symbols which represent their function and their dominant personnel. Therefore, the theological problems which arise from corporate entities are moral rather than metaphysical. Corporate identity appears to function as a behavioral referent rather than as a substantive reality.

Thus the ground is clear for developing an approach to history, based on the New Testament, in which human life is viewed as an opportunity for "remembrance"–a pattern of life which is a confession of faith and a demonstration of obedience. If the many layers of corporate identity, under which modern life is lived, are peeled away, then there remains the sovereignty of Jesus Christ over the individual. If, on the other hand, corporate entities are viewed as substantive realities ranged in hierarchy, then modern man is reduced to being at the bottom of a quasi-gnostic ladder of "angels" of descending importance, and the Lordship of Jesus Christ at the top is thoroughly obscured from the ordinary people at the bottom.

The New Testament view of history is to regard the world as a theater in which the individual can respond to the Lordship of Jesus Christ. This interest in individual response does not deny the moral importance of corporate entities, but instead declares the eternal value of the human individual.

## 2.9 Conclusion

Once the textual, lexical, and contextual problems of the word *anamnesis* are overcome, one is left, at first sight, with many open questions. There does not appear to be any prospect of ever producing the final answers to the questions of the exact nature of the Last Supper, or of the different timings of the Crucifixion in the Gospel narratives, or of the steps of development from the Last Supper to the Lord's Supper. However, if these questions could be definitely solved then the possibilty of attracting a wider spectrum of significance to the remembrance of Jesus Christ would probably be precluded. Instead, there is created the possibility of an enlarged vision of Jesus Christ which would be impossible if the matter of remembrance was reduced to a straightforward definition. If the patterns of remembrance in Judaism were transfused into Christianity then the characteristic of cultic memorials as connotating a spectrum wider than any precise reference would also have been passed on. The confessional implications of the anamnesis clause include the preeminence of Jesus Christ over all earthly authority and his Lordship over the human individual.

## NOTES

1. I Howard Marshall, **The Gospel of Luke**, (Exeter, 1978), 799-800.
2. E.g. Gregg, **Anamnesis in the Eucharist**, (Bramcote, Notts. 1976).
3. J. Jeremias, **The Eucharistic Words of Jesus**, (Oxford, 1955), 162.
4. **De Congressu Quaerendae Eruditionis Gratia**, 39; **De Virtutibus**, 176; **Legum Allegoriae**, III, 91.
5. J. W. Etheridge, "The Targums on the Pentateuch," (London, Longman Green, 1862), Vol. I, 228.
6. Cyril, Jo. 6; glaph Gen 3; hom pasch 5.7. Clement, *Paedagogica 1.5. Origen, hom* 8.6 in Gen; *hom* 8.9 in Gen.
7. G. Dix, **Jew and Greek**, (London, 1953), 101.

8. D. A. Knight, ed. **Tradition and Theology in the Old Testament**, (London, 1977), 165.

9. T. Preiss, "The Vision of History in the New Testament," in **Papers of the Ecumenical Institute No V**, (Geneva, 1950), 59-60.

# CHAPTER THREE

# An appraisal of the methodology and philosophy of the discipline of history

## 3.1 Introduction

Any discussion of anamnesis involves an implicit set of assumptions about the possibility of relating to the past. "Remembrance" implies a past, knowledge of the past, a present, and some linkage between these three within a communal apprehension. The standard modern way of relating to the past is usually comprehended under the discipline of history. Therefore, some survey of the methodology and philosophy of history is required to elucidate the nature of anamnesis. It may be that reflection on the discipline of history can contribute to the appreciation of anamnesis. It may be also that an appreciation of anamnesis can more clearly delineate the discipline of history. But it should be borne in mind that a more or less standard approach has developed by which the Bible and Christian teaching are subjected to historical criticism. The enthusiasm with which this approach has been applied has tended to obscure the limitations of the discipline of history.

Only rarely have philosophers of today investigated what is to be understood by history and what in practice historians achieve. Questions of epistemology and method have received attention to the neglect of questions about the constitution of history itself. The discipline of history has been felt to control the body of evidence that is recoverable from biblical times. Accordingly, the discipline of history has come to dominate the process of "remembrance". But, the discipline of history involves many ingredients which, when examined, prove to be so complex, that it is probably inappropriate for the discipline of history to have been used in theological studies in the way it has been used. How-

ever highly trained an historian may be, and however distinct an historical method he may appear to use, the whole rests upon a surprisingly
amorphous base. Some of the aspects of the discipline of history must
therefore be examined, and reference must be made to what historians
have written about their work.

## 3.2 Time and Historical Method

Underlying history, there is the continual flow of time. Any attempt
here to summarize scientific and philosophical views on the nature of
time would be a digression. Time, as it figures in human awareness, is
at least a common denominator in the ongoing succession of activity.
Time is usually regarded as chronological succession. And historical sequence expresses chronological succession. Now, it is commonly accepted that the development of Western civilization has required a more
conscious awareness of time in order to facilitate highly complex plan-
ning and coordination of effort. This distinctively modern awareness of
the importance of time has spilled over into the writing of history. The
minute care with which historical information is marshalled into chronological order and is therefore felt to be both manageable and comprehensible is a distinctive aspect of modern culture.

The dedicated reconstruction of the past has an extra function, however.
The development of an historical method which succeeds in making the
past as vivid as yesterday does not only impress the modern awareness
of time upon the past, but also diminishes the significance of the gap
in time between the era of any historical subject under consideration and
the present. This subtle erosion of the character of the passage of time
telescopes the interval between any historical era and the present. The
conflation of the past may reflect the triumph of modern historical
methods, but has many misleading implications. For example, to con-
ceal the passage of time could subtly turn mortality into an illusion.

By contrast, the school of logical positivism denied the reality of the
past because the past is not susceptible to empirical verification. Croce
deduced from this viewpoint that history only has reality in the mind of
the historian. This teaching goes to the opposite extreme and instead of
emphasizing the accessibility of the past, condemns the past to being
lost and irrecoverable by virtue of the passage of time and only having

any existence in historical thinking.

Certainly, time is an irreversible continuum, but there is ambiguity of time in historical study. Time is the notation of sequence in affairs, and time is the sequence within which affairs are annotated. This ambiguity raises questions as to the reality of time in perception which cannot be explored here. But any historical writing involves some explicit decision about the character of time, and the nature of the relationship between present cognition and the past.

## 3.3 "Facts" and Evidence

A further problem in historical writing is to decide on the material which is taken as the basis of historical writing. The whole of the present is composed of things from the past. The present is not a creation "ex nihilo". Therefore, the historian has to impose his own decision as to which items in the present furniture of the world are to be taken as significant for his purpose.

There is a popular fallacy that history consists of "facts". The German historian Ranke, writing in 1824, declared that his aim in writing history was "only to show what actually happened." But the enthusiasm with which many historians since the time of Ranke have mastered their sources and claimed to produce "factual" history obscures an underlying difficulty. Past history is primarily a totality consisting of everything everybody has done and everything that has ever happened to anybody. Even this statement involves the assumption that history is coextensive with human affairs. Now, plainly, most of history has been lost. The details of the overwhelming majority of the lives of men are forgotten, unknown and unrecorded. Accordingly, therefore, most of past history is unknowable and such information about the past as has survived has been through a rigorous selection process.

The severity of the selection process from which historical sources have survived is fully acknowledged by historians. War, vermin, accident, fire, earthquake, atmospheric conditions, and human carelessness are some of the many factors which have controlled the survival of historical documents, etc. Of equal importance as any of these factors, however, is human fiat. As long as chroniclers have been at work, they have been selecting which information they prefer to record. Carr has a useful illustration of the incidence of the chronicler on recorded history: "The picture of the Russian peasant as devoutly religious was destroyed by the revolution of 1917. The picture of medieval man as devoutly religious, whether true or not, is indestructible, because nearly all the known facts about him were preselected for us by people who believed it, and wanted others to believe it, and a mass of other facts, in which we might possibly have found evidence to the contrary, has been lost beyond recall."[1]

If the selection process which has controlled the survival of historical data was of uniform operation, then it could be accommodated by the uniform application of an appropriate historical method to surviving data. But any historical evidence or document is almost a random survival from the past – material whose existence in the present has been arbitrated by accident.

Any source of information about the past is a token survival from an otherwise often vanished world. Consequently, because every source has been through the selection process, every source is interpretative. And this interpretativeness of historical sources is compounded by their often being the product of an interested party. The historian has to appraise his sources and decide on their reliability. If there has been forgery, he also has to decide to which age and interest the forgery should be attributed (for example, the problem of the Donation of Constantine). The historian has to decide how to analyze his sources into usable data as well as how to construe the data.

But there is a further problem in historical research as to how historical data can be itemized. Huizinga asked, "To what extent may one isolate from the eternal flux of disparate units, specific, consistent groups as entity, as phenomena, and subject them to the intellect? In other words, in the historical world, where the smallest thing is endlessly complex, what are the units, the self-contained wholes?"[2] This question has several implications. Firstly, it is clear that further layers of interpretation are imposed by the historian if he does not content himself with simply reproducing his sources. Secondly, the fragmentation of sources into data, and the synthesis of data into written history, involve a process of destruction and recreation which may completely divorce the sources from the end product. The modern practice of the discipline of history should not be viewed as a contemporary version of the myth of the Phoenix, but historical writing is emphatically the product of the historian before it can be deemed to be the reflection of the past. Thirdly, and finally, if the past is a flux rather than a succession of discrete units, then the itemization of historical data is not necessarily the most appropriate method to discover the content of past history.

A great deal of energy has been expended on discussions as to whether history is a science. The method of science is to analyze phenomena, to classify data, and to build a general theoretical structure which accounts for the particular. Known particulars are thus subordinated to a general understanding. However, in historical research and writing there is no subordination of what is known, instead there is a co-ordination of the known. There is no system of history by which a recognizable scientific method can be followed. Schopenhauer in his essay "On History," wrote of history that: "nowhere does it know the particular by means of the universal, but it must comprehend the particular directly, and continue to creep along the ground of experience. . . ."[3]

Thus, an historian cannot fill in the gaps in his sources by applying general rules to discover unknown data. So, for example, when an historian comes to the history of the Incas, he may not feel that he has sufficient evidence for a comprehensive history or even a patchy narrative. The historian may feel that such information as exists indicates a complex of far more important factors which are quite unknown. Unless the historian wants to write an historical novel, he cannot turn incontiguous items of information into a connected narrative.

History purports to be a connected body of knowledge, methodically arrived at. The historian is confronted by momentous decisions at every stage of his work. The difficulties of recognizing the character of the meagre sources that have survived in the absence of their proper context, and of isolating usable data, almost preclude any confidence in historical writing unless it is acknowledged that it is the product of a highly developed art of informed speculation.

## 3.4 Interpretation and explanation

As has already been mentioned, in the course of historical research and writing, sources are assessed and analyzed into usable data. The problem then arises of how data are interpreted. Some information is discarded; some data are given a low value, and some given a high value. A hierarchy of understanding emerges which invests each individual datum with relative significance. Thus the plan of eighteenth century English economic history is dominated by the grand concepts of the agricultural and industrial revolutions. Various subsidiary schemes form the parts of these overall concepts, and so take account of technical innovation, the development of trade, population movements, improvements in transport, the impact of war, capital accumulation, and such like.

Schemata of historical understanding have been described as "colligatory concepts."[4] These concepts function as summary descriptions of past periods, and also imply a pattern of historical events. For example, "revolt" implies an uprising, a fair measure of violence, and an attempt to change a government. Colligatory concepts have to be tailored to fit the facts, and should also illuminate the situation. However, there are difficulties with colligatory concepts which mean that they have to be used carefully. A decision about the character of an era can control the selection of data from that era which then reinforce the character, whereas it would be more correct for the character of an era to emerge from the sources which survive. Also, an historian has to bear in mind the possible risks of offering as a schema of understanding a description of a period which would have been unrecognizable to the people of that time.

History cannot have a merely descriptive function. All history is interpretative, and therefore has an explanatory function as well. Marrou has written that: "explanation in history is the discovery, the comprehension, the analysis of a thousand ties which, in a possibly inextricable fashion, unite the many faces of human reality one to the other. These ties bind each phenomenon to neighboring phenomena, each state to previous ones, immediate or remote (and in like manner to their results). One may rightfully ask oneself if real history is not just that: the concrete experience of the complexity of truth . . ."[5]

In the absence of any possibility of quasi-scientific empirical data in history, the historian works in a flux of interpretation and explanation. There can be no objectivity of fact in history. Indeed Carr has written that: "The concept of absolute truth is . . . not appropriate to the world of history."[6] The only objectivity that Carr will tolerate in history is that of the relation between fact and interpretation. The distinction between "fact" and "interpretation" is thereby underlined. Facts may once have had an empirically verifiable existence, but any present knowledge can only be interpretation.

"Facts" and "interpretation" have an approximate parallel in German historiography in the terms "Geschichte" and "Historie". The word "Geschichte" has the sense of occurrence, while "Historie" refers to the investigation and reporting of individual events. However, whilst this distinction can be recognized, the distinction cannot be drawn clearly. Historical facts can only be recognized if they are given significance and interpreted. Any one detail that is picked out from the colossal detail of everyday life is interpreted simply in the act of being picked out. The main sources of information about past history arise from documents and excavations, and it would be awkward to say which are the more difficult to interpret.

Isolated data cannot be boldly presented as history. Thus the beheading of Charles Stuart on its own is meaningless. But once the background of seventeenth century English history is apprehended, the beheading of Charles Stuart acquires meaning and significance. Furthermore, an historical datum can be given a different significance in different contexts. Thus the beheading of Charles I is given a different significance in a history of the belief in the "divine right of kings," as against a fiscal history of England in the Seventeenth Century, as against a history of capital punishment in Europe since the time of Charlemagne.

It would appear that all extant historical sources are at the mercy of historians to derive what they will from their research. However, there is a differentiation which has already been alluded to as between "known history" and "unknown history"—that is, as between the fragments of historical information that have survived and the totality of past history. The distinction between fragmentary history and the sum of past history is important. "Known history" is made up of interpreted data extracted from arbitrarily surviving historical sources. "Unknown history" is made up of a continual flux, within which discrete events are submerged.

It may be felt that it is right to be suspicious of the more inventive patterns of historical interpretation and explanation. However, if historians did not have the courage of their convictions then no history would be written. The limitations of historical sources demand the use of colligatory concepts, otherwise historical writing would be impossible. The absence of the reality of historical fact in "known history" entails an interpretative art.

## 3.5 Progress

One of the models of history that particularly appeals to people's susceptibilities is that of "Progress." Progress carries a remarkable explanatory force and has connotations which almost automatically command allegiance. Progress appeals to popular optimism and expectations for the future. There is no one formula for identifying or defining progress. Instead, it appears that progress is a pattern of historical interpretation. Cultural change has often been described in terms of technical innovation (eg. the "Bronze Age," or the "Iron Age"), and progress can carry weight as a moral justification for technical change.

Ideas of progress are rooted in the accepted fact of the accumulation of knowledge, and the assurance that given modern university research programmes, etc., knowledge will continue to accumulate. The greatest evidence of progress is usually conceded to be man's control of his environment. Goudzwaard has considered the provenance of ideas of progress, and has traced the deliberate pursuit of progress back to the Renaissance. Goudzwaard has written that: "Renaissance man ventured into the world around him to discover it and to subject it to himself. This domination ideal of western humanism – the will to rational knowledge and domination of the world in every respect: scientific, artistic, political, technical, and economic – was already at that time inextricably linked with . . . the freedom or personality ideal of humanism, that is the effort to develop an absolutely free, autonomous personality." "The domination and personality ideals belong together. What would express the freedom of the human personality better than man's knowledge, control and domination of the world? How else could the domination ideal be realized except on the basis of the free, unfettered development of human personality?"[7]

The inspiration of the ideals of the Renaissance certainly can be reckoned to have left an enduring impress on Western society. However, Goudzwaard has pointed out that these two ideals confront each other in opposition. The "world" includes people. The more people that exercise domination, the more they are likely to overlap. So progress inevitably connotes competition. Furthermore, there is no barrier to forestall domination being exercised by one person over other people–and then the dominated are no longer free to realize their personalities "unfettered." The ideals of progress presume that every man is an island – an impossible basis for society; and every island a world – a delusion only realizable in solipsism.

It would appear, therefore, that progress is a defective view of history as well as a potentially disastrous rationale of motivation in society. Progress and its index – success – may function in popular thought as the legitimation of change and endeavor, but also focusses historical significance on particular aspects of the historical process, and may dismiss as secondary the events of history which do not contribute to change. History as the record of "progress" is a very partial approach to history. If progress were to be adopted as the key to history, then a great deal of evidence as to social stagnation and cultural regress would have to be overlooked.

It can never be known whether "progress" is the prelude of future triumph or catastrophe, but progress does focus attention on change and it would seem to be dangerous if an emphasis on progress has dimmed the significance of social stability. Schopenhauer, having embraced Eastern philosophy, had a peculiarly detached view of history and felt that "history is to be regarded as the rational self-consciousness of the human race; it is to the race what the reflected and connected consciousness, conditioned by the faculty of reason, is to the individual."[8] But the emphasis on progress has bred a sense of discontinuity with the past – institutions are no longer legitimized by the past alone, but increasingly by their present and future efficacy and utility. Progress may be believed to have an exhortative value in society, but in the context of the philosophy of history, "progress" is of protest value only against the immeasurable vastness of unknown history.

This discussion of "progress" illustrates the problems of embracing any pattern of interpretation in historical writing.

## 3.6 The Historian and History

A further factor in the writing of history is the historian himself. The historian has the key role in the writing of history. The historian is virtually a prism who refracts the past and reveals its constituent elements. Obviously, character is variable between different historians, even historians who have been trained to follow the same historical method. And the character of an historian controls what that historian "sees" in the past. Marrou wrote that: "From the point of view of the theory of knowledge, history appears as an inextricable mixture of subject and object. The truth that is actually accessible to us is restricted by the particular, and therefore distorted, view which results from the historian's own personality and mental structures, his cultural background, and his curiosity, which determine the form of his questions and the elaboration of the answers he finds."[9]

If history is an art, then the personalities of historians are an integral part of historical writing. Historians confront their research material as individuals. Dilthey launched a school of historical method which envisaged an empathy with historical data through the exercise of historical imagination. In this way, Dilthey aspired to enter into the fabric of meaning that existed in any given era and locality. "What man has done, thought, and created, he believed, man can understand. By extending our understanding both to individuals, who are the only real units in history and to the man-made – and, therefore comprehensible – context in which they stand, we grasp the historical world as meaningful. By thus recapturing . . . the meaning which individuals, here and there, have perceived in and attributed to their circumstances, the meaning which informed their actions and became embodied in their creations, the historian can tell a meaningful story."[10]

These views of Dilthey have found their more modern parallel in the ideas of Collingwood. This deliberately subjective approach Collingwood explained as follows: "To the historian, the activities whose history he is studying are not spectacles to be watched, but experiences to be lived through in his own mind; they are objective, or known to him, only because they are also subjective, or activities of his own."[11]

However, it has to be asked whether constructive retrospection is a live option in historical study. It is laudable for an historian to be deeply involved with his work, but a feat of imagination should not be equated with a reconstructed past. The historian must not cross the bridge from being an artist to being an illusionist. An excessive reliance on imagination would remove the limitations which history depends on to be an art.

## 3.7 The Meaning of History

One factor which has often affected historical writing is a conviction that history has an overall significance. This is a larger issue than interpretation in historical writing. Interpretation is employed on a small canvas, but the meaning of history is concerned with the significance of the whole panorama of the past.

The discussions that have taken place as to a meaning of the known historical process can broadly be classified under two alternative viewpoints. Known history can be regarded as having either a transcendent meaning or an immanent meaning. Any transcendent meaning is to do with a purpose that is beyond history, whilst any immanent meaning may be discerned within history. An example of an immanent meaning of history is that ascribed in the teachings of dialectical materialism.

The usual way in which the meaning of history is discussed is in terms of teleology – history is understood in terms of purpose. There are immanent teleologies such as in Eastern convictions of karma, or in Western views of process theology. Transcendent teleologies are often easily traceable in Western religious outlooks on history. The view that purpose is imposed from "outside" the world, and that every person and thing exists to achieve a specific goal is fairly widespread. The belief that everything and everyone is ranged in a single overall plan is not foreign to many Christian believers. But such a viewpoint can amount to a prejudice, because for the teleological thinker all unintelligible disorder, disaster, and suffering, are due not to the nature of things but are only unintelligible because we do not yet know their purpose. "Teleology is a form of faith capable of neither confirmation nor refutation by any kind of experience; the notions of evidence, proof, probability and so on, are wholly inapplicable to it."[12]

Whilst it is desirable that in written history episodes and eras may have distinctive characters or meanings, this is not an open gateway through which to enter into the search for the significance of known history as a whole. Danto has remarked that: "There are wider and narrower contexts, but history as a whole is plainly the widest possible such context, and to ask the meaning of the whole of history is to deprive oneself of the contextual frame within which such requests are intelligible."[13] Indeed, Danto is reluctant to allow significance to be ascribed to even the total past, and insists that the question be asked of a totality of past, present, and future. He then points out that as the future has not happened yet, it is impossible to arrive at any overall significance to history.

Butterfield understood what he described as "the cry for an interpretation of the human drama," and realized that this longing could not be met by writing from within the discipline of history. Rather he suggested that this heartfelt cry can be met only by something more like prophecy.

All things considered, it is very difficult to accord any overall significance to known history. Historical data may be given relative significance in historical writing, but there is no necessary overall meaning to known history. Indeed, it would be very surprising if there were any overall meaning to known history, because known history is extremely fragmentary. Accordingly, therefore, known history can give no clue to the meaning, if any, of the totality of the past, let alone a clue to the meaning of the totality of the past, the present, and the future.

## 3.8  The Existence of the Past

To state that past history is a great unknown of which we have relatively few indications in surviving historical data is to admit that the events of history are unknowable. One can know facts through their interpretation, but the events of history are past and are not subject to direct examination. However, to call past history "unknown" also contains an implicit admission that the past in some way exists. The question has to be faced as to the kind of existence which belongs to the content of the past.

This problem has been evaded in the discussion of the philosophy of history, although this question is fundamental to the endeavor of historical writing. Indeed, it could be that ignoring this problem could vitiate historical research and writing. If an historian claims to reproduce the past and has failed to take account of the way in which the past exists, he may misrepresent entirely the nature of his work. However, the only writer who has been greatly exercised by this matter has been H. D. Oakeley.

Oakeley was provoked to consider this problem by an observation by C. D. Broad that: "once an event has happened, it exists eternally."[15] Oakeley defined the past as: "a series of events having a once-for-all or never-to-be-repeated character, and an irreversible order, together with the negative character attaching to non-presentness."[16] She clearly distinguished the question of the existence of the past from the interpretation that the past endures and is real in the present. Furthermore, she felt that the past exists regardless of our ignorance about it: "the existence of the past would not seem to be affected by the question of our knowledge of any particular content of past history, or the truth of our judgements concerning it, or the question whether it can be discovered in the present."[17] Oakeley anticipated the difficulties of the ideas on history of Collingwood. Oakeley insisted that the past is past, and that the data of history cannot be resuscitated neither resurrected nor resumed in a "Now" to which they do not belong.

Whilst it is a common convention that the present exists, the question arises as to what happens to the existence of the present as it becomes past. Oakeley cites Broad as saying that: "nothing has happened to the present by becoming past, except that fresh slices of existence have been added to the total history of the world."[18] Oakeley eventually found herself driven to deduce the existence of the past from the general human experience of the passage of time. Oakeley declared that: "The affirmation that the past is real . . . is a mental necessity, through which is provided the *a priori* required for history."[19] She thus found the reality of the past tied to the reality of the present.

All this highlights the obstacles to any direct knowledge of the past. Certainly, any interpretative certitude is precluded from historical writing. The past is not susceptible to investigation. Therefore, historical writing rests on evidence that has been "left behind" in the present. So if the pastness of the past is taken seriously, historical writing can have no direct bearing on the past at all. One can only say of the past that: "it exists, but it is veiled from direct perception." Historical writing can probably only claim to be the shadow of the reality of history.

## 3.9 The Past and Tradition

There is a great difference between an investigation of the problems of known history and the way that the past affects traditional societies. In a primitive society, the past "operates most powerfully upon its present behavior, but the past is taken up into the present in the form of traditionally determined custom. The past operates upon the present by way of habits of the group rather than as a formulated group memory."[20] The habits of a primitive society effectively remember the past, whereas anything of "factual" nature before the recent past apart from the genealogies may be forgotten.

It may be affirmed that there is in custom an evaluation of the past. Much tradition is non-verbal custom – tradition perpetuated in behavior. Therefore, traditionally determined behavior implicitly affirms the reality of the past, and also allows the innate significance of a past that is directly unknown to be expressed.

The study of the way that oral tradition functions has absorbed many lifetimes of work. It appears that oral tradition is the verbal counterpart of traditionally determined custom. Oral tradition, therefore, also mediates an unknown past. Oral tradition may include information about past events, but such details are often incidental to its main purpose which is apparently to present a digest of the significance of past experience and to set a context for living which may be held by common convention.

Tradition sidesteps historical methodology and may more clearly reveal the meaning of the past and the innate significance of particular events. Indeed, tradition may claim to envisage the whole of reality as being dominated by particular events. Obviously, as tradition is of far more complicated provenance than most historical sources, it attracts its own disciplines. Tradition may be limited by geography and many other factors, but tradition is, nevertheless, a digest of an "unknown" past.

Hayek has written that: "most of the rules of conduct which govern our actions, and most of the institutions which arise out of this regularity, are adaptations to the impossibility of anyone taking conscious account of all the particular facts which enter into the order of society."[21] The past may play a bigger role even in modern civilization than it may be given credit for, albeit through highly attenuated tradition.

Tradition, therefore, may be viewed as offering a far more obvious relationship with the past than the discipline of history. Tradition is not dependent on the accidental survival of historical evidence. However, the analysis and comprehension of oral traditions have not yet been stabilized.

## 3.10 Implications for historical method in Biblical Theology

Various aspects of the discipline of history may be called upon in biblical theology. The variety of approaches to the writing of history colors the writing of biblical theology, as illustrated by a few examples in the following paragraphs.

One of the most conspicuous uses of the discipline of history to condition the fabric of biblical theology has been that of Bultmann. Bultmann wrote that, "the modern study of history . . . does not take into account any intervention of God or of the devil or of demons in the course of history. Instead, the course of history is considered to be an unbroken whole, complete in itself, though differing from the course of nature because there are in history spiritual powers which influence the will of persons. Granted that not all historical events are determined by physical necessity and that persons are responsible for their actions, nevertheless nothing happens without rational motivation."[22] Bultmann appeals to the discipline of history as reason for engaging in the "demythologizing" of the Christian gospel. However, it would appear that Bultmann has misapplied the discipline of history, and imagined that history is a science with general principles that can dictate its content. In fact, history was made for man, not man for history; and the religious experience of mankind is part of the past and cannot be jettisoned. Whilst Bultmann was entitled to pursue any pattern of interpretation of history that he chose, it was no legitimation to call it "modern", with the concomitant echoes of progress.

Eichrodt has written that the concern of the theology of the Old Testament is "to construct a complete picture of the Old Testament realm of belief, in other words to comprehend in all its uniqueness and immensity what is, strictly speaking, the proper object of Old Testament study."[23] Eichrodt may be said to have followed the method of Dilthey and Collingwood in trying to enter the past by dint of exercising a theologically conditioned historical imagination - to try to appreciate the past from "inside," as it were, rather than to evaluate it from the distance of time.

By contrast, von Rad regards the Hexateuch and the Deuteronomistic history in the Old Testament as a "saving history that is drawn up by faith, and is accordingly confessional in character."[24] And von Rad affirms that the subject of Old Testament theology "cannot be a systematically ordered "world of faith" of Israel or of the really overwhelming vitality and creative productivity of Jahwism, for the world of faith is not the subject of these testimonies which Israel raised to Jahweh's action in history.[25] Consequently, von Rad suggests that: "If . . . we put Israel's picture of her history in the forefront of our theological consideration, we encounter what appropriately is the most essential subject of a theology of the Old Testament . . . "[26] That is to say that biblical theology has to be related more to tradition than to the critical history of Israel–to Israel's self-understanding than to a modern conjecture as to how that self-understanding arose. The embracing of tradition is fundamental to its appreciation, and von Rad has emphasized that this is as legitimate an enterprise as the construction of a critical history of Israelite traditions.

Ladd defines biblical theology as "the description and interpretation of the divine activity within the scene of human history that seeks man's redemption."[27] Thus, biblical theology may be acknowledged as an interpretative art, akin to history but dealing with traditional material rather than with historical data.

The presuppositions about history that are embraced in biblical theology control the approach of the theologian to the biblical narratives. The great variety of approaches, a few of which have been illustrated in this section, each has a contribution to make to the overall perspective of the Judaeo-Christian spectrum of faith. However, it must be considered as to whether some historical methods may be wholly inappropriate in dealing with some biblical material. But it could be that until tradition, in all its dynamism, is understood, biblical theology will continue to be at the mercy of the historical presuppositions of theologians.

## 3.11 "Known" History and the "Unknown" Past

A distinction has accrued between "known" history and "unknown" history which must now be clarified. Surviving historical evidence is no more than the shadow of the past in the present. The past is unknown and unknowable. Whilst traditions may count as historical evidence, they offer a digest of the past. Historical writing, however, can only deal with evidence that has survived an arbitrary selection process and has, as it were, been left behind in the present.

The discipline of history has been tailored to the nature of historical evidence. It is inappropriate, therefore, to apply historical methods to tradition. The Biblical writings are primarily traditional and secondarily historical. This is inevitably the case as the Biblical writings were the deposit of believing communities in which traditions were geared to use. Just as the faithful came to control the canon of scripture through consensus, so the common life of the faithful may be suggested to be the framework within which the content of the Biblical traditions was determined. Certainly, the discipline of history can neither control nor regulate the practice of anamnesis.

It has been demonstrated that historical writing is incapable of pronouncing definitively on the meaning, if any, of the past – known or unknown. The historian marshalls his evidence, such as it is, in detachment from the continuous flux of the past. Only tradition can take account of the subtle modulations inherent in the past from which it emerges. Tradition is molded by the events themselves, as opposed to historical writing which is founded on such evidence as might survive.

Modern historical writing cannot control religious faith, but can only be regarded as a demonstration of the existence of historical evidence. The material to be found in tradition is not in itself an object of faith, but is part and parcel of a way of life. Known history is but the shadow of the past. Unknown history is a totality that can only be encountered by becoming immersed in a living tradition.

# NOTES

1. Carr, **What is History?** (Harmondsworth, Middlesex, 1973), 14.
2. Huizinga, "The Idea of History," in ed. F. Stern, **The Varieties of History**, (London, 1970), 290.
3. Schopenhauer: **The World as Will and Representation**, (New York, 1966), Vol. II, 439-440.
4. Walsh, "Colligatory Concepts in History" in ed. P. Gardiner, **The Philosophy of History**, (London, 1974).
5. Marrou, **The Meaning of History**, (Dublin, 1966), 192.
6. Carr, **What is History?** 120.
7. Goudzwaard, **Capitalism and Progress**, (Toronto, 1979), 155.
8. Schopenhauer, **The World as Will and Representation**, (New York, 1966), Vol. II, 445.
9. Marrou, **Time and Timeliness**, (New York, 1969), 57.
10. Rickman, **Meaning in History**, W. Dilthey's thoughts on History and Society, (London, 1961), 61-62.
11. Collingwood, **The Idea of History**, (New York, 1956), 128.
12. Berlin, **Historical Inevitability**, (London, 1955), 17.
13. Danto, **Analytical Philosophy of History**, (London, 1968), 13.
14. Butterfield, **Christianity and History**, (London, 1950), 24.
15. Quoted by Oakeley, "The Status of the Past" in **Proceedings of the Aristotelian Society**, Vol. XXXII, (London, 1932), 228.
16. Ibid., 232-233.
17. Ibid., 234.
18. Ibid., 238.
19. Ibid., 242.
20. M.M. Lewis, **Language in Society**, (London, 1947), 112.

21. Hayek, **Law, Legislation and Liberty**, (London, 1973), Vol. I, 13.

22. Bultmann, **Jesus Christ and Mythology**, (New York, 1958), 15, 16.

23. Eichrodt, **Theology of the Old Testament**, (London, 1975), Vol. I, 25.

24. Von Rad, **Old Testament Theology**, (London, 1975), Vol. I, 107.

25. Ibid., 111.

26. Ibid., 112.

27. Ladd, **A Theology of the New Testament**, (London, 1975), 26.

# CHAPTER FOUR

# The Theology of History

## 4.1 The Understanding of History in the Early Church

The Christian Church and the Roman Empire often had an uneasy relationship, but the general impression may be painted that the opinion grew in the Church that the united Roman Empire existed under the providence of God for the propagation of the Gospel. As the estimation of the Roman Empire developed the Empire was accorded an important place in the divine plan of salvation. Eusebius of Caesarea was the extreme exponent of this approach to history and even went as far as applying messianic categories to the rule of the Roman emperors.

History was viewed as a progress from Creation to Judgment in which the hand of God could be clearly discerned. It was unquestioned that God controlled world affairs and could use one nation to scourge another in punishment. Augustine himself, until the beginning of the fifth century accepted contemporary ideas about the course of history and the evaluation of the Roman Empire. Then in 410, Alaric entered Rome and the city was sacked. Part of the reaction which this disaster produced was that pagans surmised that because the ancient cults had been neglected in favor of Christianity, the pagan deities had withdrawn their protection from the city. Christianity was therefore responsible for the sack of Rome. Augustine's book, *City of God*, was intended to be an answer to these accusations.

## 4.2 The Teaching of Augustine

Augustine developed an individual approach to the significance of history. Augustine thought the importance that had been attached to Rome was quite erroneous, and showed that he thought that within the entire conspectus of history a mere city is not of great significance. The Roman Empire, for Augustine, was just one among the many Empires of history.

In the *City of God* there is no effort to interpret Roman history in prophetic categories. Instead, Roman history is regarded as part of world history. Augustine ascribed "to the true God alone the power to grant kingdoms and empires" (V. 21), and thought that: "the same God gave power to Marius and to Gaius Caesar, to Augustus and to Nero, to the Vespasians, father and son, the most attractive emperors, as well as to Domitian, the most ruthless tyrant; and . . . the same God gave the throne to Constantine the Christian, and also to Julian the Apostate." (V. 21).

The polarity of Augustine's work between the earthly and the heavenly enabled him to have a measure of detachment towards Rome. Rome became dispensable, and God's purposes did not stand or fall with any particular civilization. In the *City of God* Augustine reflects on the appallingly checkered career of Rome and he makes nonsense of any claim that Rome received any divine favors in return for services rendered.

Augustine wrote that: "While this Heavenly City . . . is on pilgrimage in this world, she calls out citizens from all nations and so collects a society of aliens, speaking all languages " (XIX.17). "It is completely irrelevant to the Heavenly City what dress is worn or what manner of life adopted by each person who follows the faith that is the way to God, provided that these do not conflict with the divine instructions." (XIX.19). Augustine recognized the dangers of linking the Church to anything temporal that might be discarded. Thus, if the Church had been tied to the Empire, then the Church would have been bound to the Empire's political perpetuation, and any failure of the Empire would mean the failure of the mission of the Church. Augustine withheld from the Empire and every other secular institution any ultimate significance. Within universal history he distinguished the Biblical history which alone unambiguously revealed God's hand. But otherwise he felt that there was no privileged insight by which to judge anything historical.

In the midst of the complexity of human life, Augustine did not believe the judgment of God to be absent, but untraceable (XX.2). Whilst Augustine was convinced that God was in control of history, yet its meaning was hidden until the Last Day. The vision of the ambiguity of history, emanating from a time of crisis, has valuable lessons. It was unfortunate that, perhaps because Augustine did not present a clear and systematic account of his views, this teaching was not taken up by subsequent writers.

## 4.3 Augustine's teaching neglected; Reaction against traditional historiography

Augustine's disciple, Orosius, did not imitate his master and with his *Seven Books of Histories Against the Pagans* reverted to the tradition of Eusebius. This trend of historical writing and appreciation by which God's hand was revealed in history, rather than his judgment being hidden, eventually foundered on the rising tide of Renaissance thought. Machiavelli represents in extreme the tendency to deviate from traditional historiography and was of the opinion that a writer of history should have no religion at all so as to avoid bias.

The implications of the way in which Augustine turned from traditional historiography have not been exploited in Christian historical writing. Instead it has continued to be held by many Christian writers that God's will is manifested in world affairs. It is interesting how Popper protested against this viewpoint: "it is often considered a Christian dogma that God reveals Himself in history; that history has meaning; and that its meaning is the purpose of God . . . I contend that this view is pure idolatry and superstition . . ." "To maintain that God reveals Himself in what is usually called "history," in the history of international crime and mass murder, is indeed blasphemy; for what really happens within the realm of human lives is hardly ever touched upon by this cruel and at the same time childish affair." "The theory that God reveals Himself and His judgement in history is indistinguishable from the theory that worldly success is the ultimate judge and justification of our actions."[1]

Popper thought political history to be so dependent upon human interests that it was impossible to deduce evidence of the will of God from historical writing. Popper recognized a vivid contrast between the reality of everyday life and the artificiality of written history.

## 4.4 The Christian View of History

In the anthology, *God, History and Historians* edited by McIntire, an item by Latourette is included.[2] Latourette discussed the Christian view of history and considered the following features to be especially significant:

    i.   a perspective and a set of values which are the reverse of those which mankind generally esteems;

    ii.  the individual is of outstanding importance;

    iii. cultural and institutional factors are reduced to a backdrop for person-to-person relationships;

    iv. time and history are surrounded by eternity.

It should be noted that such an approach as that advocated by Latourette precludes any historical synthesis or generalization. It was synthesis that produced the "synthetic" or "artificial" history about which Popper complained.

The four qualities which Latourette isolated are reflected in the Bible. It has been fashionable to regard the Bible as an historical work – as recording part of the whole succession of events in the world – but this is to overlook the fact that the Christian view of history is quite different from the normal approach to history. There has been such preoccupation with the "historicity" of events narrated in the Bible – whether they actually happened – that their special character has been obscured. It is surely inconsistent to expect Biblical narratives to be subject to the same canons of historical criticism as ordinary historical documents when conventional historical methodology is geared to producing history which is diametrically opposed to what has been delineated as the Christian view of history. As has already been affirmed, the Biblical narratives have a far more complicated provenance than historical documents, and require a different approach.

The temptation to assimilate the Bible to conventional history may have been felt to make the Bible more "relevant", but the result of handling traditional material in this way is to distance it from everyday life.

The way in which selectivity operates in the writing of history has already been demonstrated, and the grand themes of history which an historian uses to give continuity and comprehensibility to even social history can never reconstruct the complex of everyday life in any area. Certainly the biblical record is a source of historical evidence which fits in with the records of Egypt, Assyria, Babylon, Persia, Greece and Rome. But world affairs are only a backcloth in the Bible. The main focus of interest in the Bible is the dealings and relationship between God and men, and these dealings are mediated by tradition rather than by history.

## 4.5 The "Heilsgeschichte" View Rejected

It has been the view of some scholars that given the historicity of leading Biblical events, a chain of events could be listed in a sequence by which the salvation of believers had been effected. This pattern of understanding has been called the "Heilsgeschichte" School. The idea that there is a "Salvation-History" took root in German theology, and relied for its legitimation on a mixture of historical and theological discipline. Dodd followed German theology in distiguishing between "sacred history" and "secular history", and felt that: "It was important to bear in mind that the same events enter into sacred and secular history; the events are the same, but they form two distinguishable series."[3]

Dodd accepted that: "There are innumerable things that happen, in the sense that they have a definite locus in time and space, but no one is sufficiently interested in them to remember or record them."[4] But Dodd went on to say that: "Such occurrences do not constitute history." "History in the full sense consists of events which possess not merely a private but a public interest, and a meaning which is related to broad and permanent concerns of human society."[5] Dodd missed the significance of the unkown past, and assimilated the treatment of biblical narratives to historical methodology rather than to the more problematic evaluation of traditions emerging from the "unknown past". The "broad and permanent concerns of human society" are the grand theories of history distanced from the details of everday life. The "unknown past", like the Bible, is primarily made up of details which are overlooked by conventional history.

It appears that Dodd further obscures his position when he affirms that "there is another series into which historical events may fall, that which I have called "sacred history," or history as a process of redemption and revelation. Of this series the biblical history forms the inner core. But the Bible always assumes that the meaning of this inner core is the ultimate meaning of all history, since God is the Maker and Ruler of all mankind, who created all things for Himself, and redeemed the world to Himself. That is to say, the whole history is in the last resort sacred history . . . ."[6] This attempt to relate biblical history to world history, fails because it depends on a false polarity between insufficiently clarified categories. The polarity "sacred history"–"secular history" is scarcely an adequate analysis of the problem. Whilst this polarity as employed by Dodd does justice to the ambiguity of the world process, the "pastness" of the past is thoroughly disregarded. Dodd himself wrote that: "The best historian of the past is one who has so familiarized himself with his period that he can feel and judge its significance as from within."[7] And what Dodd expects of the historian, he also expects of a believer: "in its central sacrament the Church places itself ever anew within the eschatological crisis in which it had its origin. Here Christ is set before us incarnate, crucified, and risen, and we partake of the benefits of His finished work, as contemporaries with it. We are neither merely recalling a story out of the past, nor merely expressing and nourishing a hope for the future, but experiencing in one significant rite the reality of the coming of Christ . . . It is this that gives character to the Church, that it lives always, when it is its most real self, within the historical moment of its redemption."[8] Dodd continues even more emphatically about the eucharist: " . . . that which the Church experiences is not just an eternal reality set forth under the forms of space, time and matter. It is a slice of the actual history of the world – something that happened "sub Pontio Pilato". It happened – and we are 'there'."[9]

This evasion of the reality of the passage of time is really very disturbing. If there was the implication that this approach was just a way of highlighting the importance of the salvific events, then such poetic license would be unexceptionable. But deliberately to hold that some sort of telescoping of the passage of time can take place is unwarranted.

It is equally disturbing to turn to Cullmann's writings and find him declaring that: "All the worship that we hear about in the Bible makes the past and future present."[10] This extraordinary assertion again masks the passage of time—and if time is an aspect of God's creation then surely the worship of Almighty God should take account of the way creation has been organized. Cullmann's assertion, which he presents as being representative of modern scholarship, is all the more extraordinary in view of the way the Bible itself emphasizes the passage of time, especially as the narrative portions of the Bible are built around the simple fact of the passage of time. Anachronism is not a proper basis for worship.

Cullmann is careful to assert that: "The eph hapax, the once-for-all character of the various Christ events of salvation history may not be given up,"[11] and further states that: "the problem of the relationship between eph hapax and the presentation of the past is ultimately that of salvation history itself . . . ."[12]

Cullmann is possibly in rather more of a cleft stick than he admits. He appears anxious about the possibility of relating to ancient events and cannot avoid somehow telescoping the present and the past. Cullmann completes the circle of his thought and says of the death of Jesus Christ: "Although its 'once-for-all-ness' must not be jeopardized by the thought of a repetition, we must still refer here to the present, real experience of the past in the anamnesis . . ."[13] At this point in the text, Cullmannn uses a footnote to refer readers to Leenhardt's book *Ceci est mon corps*, presumably to gain clarification of meaning. However, when the appropriate page is reached, the reader finds that remembrance means: "the restoration of a past situation which has for the moment disappeared. To remember is to make present actual. Thanks to this 'remembrance' time does not unfold in a straight line, adding irrevocably one upon another the periods of which it is composed. The past and the present are mingled."[14]

This remarkable understanding of remembrance which is imputed to the Israelites implies that they suffered from an equally remarkable credulity. Remembrance, as has already been demonstrated, is considerably motivated by a confessional intention. Remembrance involves an evaluation of the past, not an attempt to circumvent the passage of time.

If it is possible to feel that salvific events of the past are encountered in some way in the present, then it is reasonable to ask for some clarification as to what is being encountered. Thus Dodd explains the preaching of the Church as: "a re-presentation of the history of Jesus: it is designed to place the hearers in the very present of the historical event."[15] If it could be possible to encounter or experience past events, then opportunities would arise for critical verification, and traditions would become history. If Christianity were based on historical writings rather than narrative traditions, faith would be at a much lower premium. If the tenets of faith could be proved by some process of "remembrance" doubt would have vanished long ago. The "Heilsgeschichte" view of salvation-history cannot offer a satisfactory understanding of remembrance.

## 4.6  The Discipline of History and the experience of faith

Christian apologetic has come to lean heavily on an appeal to historical evidence. A modern example is not difficult to find: "Once disprove the historicity of Jesus Christ, and Christianity will collapse like a pack of cards. For it all depends on this fundamental conviction, that God was made manifest in human flesh. And that is a matter, not of ideology or mythology but history."[16] However, such an appeal is deceptively simple, and does not take account of the problems inherent in historical method. Futhermore, such an affirmation opens the possibilities that not only is the Christian faith dependent upon history, but even that theology is an interpretation of history.

Harvey has explored the possibility of history allowing faith to exist, and found the relationship between history and faith to be rather a convoluted affair. Historical evidence would seem to be inimical to faith. If the basis of faith was historical evidence, then Christianity would fall victim to its own teaching: "It was . . . Christianity which taught the world that God is truth and truth, divine, and it was Christianity which held aloft the ideal that one should be prepared to sacrifice everything in the service of this divinity. If men took seriously this will-to-truth and embraced everything which seemed to safeguard it, then Nietzsche felt it was no exaggeration to say that Christianity as dogma perished of its own morality."[17]

It is very difficult to rescue faith from this argument unless it is accepted that faith is not controlled by historical evidence. If a thorough-going historico-critical approach to the leading salvific events is thought to challenge faith, then the question needs to be asked as to what historical truth is as a goal. It has already been shown that there is no absolute truth to be achieved in historical studies, and the sheer impossibility of ever meeting historical criticism completely is a reminder that Christians were exhorted to the remembrance of Jesus Christ, not to a clinically verified historical certitude.

All this is not to deny the way that biblical traditions emphasize the "event-character" as salvific events, but there is a challenge to the way that historical questions have often dominated the appraisal of biblical material. It is commonly recognized that Christianity is uniquely historical for it is wholly dependent for its credibility on certain events which are alleged to have taken place during a particular period of one week in Palestine nearly two thousand years ago. So there is a sense in which Christianity is open to being shown to be false. But Mascall is not shy of some far larger questions: "What . . . is the link between my existence here and now in London and the thing that happened in Palestine so long ago and about which I read in the Gospels? How do I know that the Christ of my present experience and the Christ of the Gospels are the same person? How, indeed, do I know that the Christ of the Gospels is a genuine historical figure at all? And why does it matter whether he is or not?"[18]

These questions set out the dimensions of the problem far more clearly. Mascall also explores the pitfalls of trying to link the present with an increasingly remote era: ". . . even if critical scholarship proved beyond all doubt the accuracy of the biblical account . . . it still could not prove that this first-century teacher was the Saviour whose power and love I experience today." "Even if I had the most vivid experience of the intervention of a loving Saviour in my own life, it would still be a mere act of decision on my part that identified him with the Jesus of the Gospels, rather than, for example, with Gautama Buddha. The only way out would be to ascribe to the act of faith a strictly magical character, as enabling me to by-pass the temporal process altogether; but for this I can see no warrant."[19]

Mascall feels that the solution to this problem of the identification of

Christ today with the Christ of the Gospels is to be found in the Church as the extension through the centuries of the Incarnation. The view has considerable attractiveness but it is a solution which is inappropriate to the particular problem which Mascall is addressing. Granted that there is a continuity in the life of the Church reaching back to Jesus Christ, there is still the problem as to how to relate from the "now" to the "then".

A. M. Ramsey has described the Church as "a community of experience reaching across the generations so that the language of symbolism which it uses can evoke the past in a way which strikes a chord in the experience of the present."[20] This elegant description takes account of the passage of time and represents a course of argument that has been carefully steered between the Scylla of saying that the past is totally irrecoverable and the Charybdis of saying that the past can be conjured up in the present. However, when Ramsey tries to forge a more definite linkage between the past and the experience of the present generation, he affirms that: "Through the centuries the living past has been realised in Christian experience, for it is the work of the Holy Spirit to reproduce it in its dynamic power."[21] But it is scarcely a satisfactory solution to resolve a philosophical problem by invoking the third Person of the Holy Trinity. To attempt in this way to use the doctrine of God to smooth over problems raised by philosophical reflection is an application of the much discredited "God-of-the-gaps" solution whereby anything that cannot be accounted for is ascribed to the operation of God.

Collingwood's theory of historical understanding, which has already been referred to, in terms of which: "Historical knowledge is the knowledge of what mind has done in the past, and at the same time it is the redoing of this, the perpetuation of past acts in the present . . ." has been a frequent resort for those dealing with the problem of the presence of the past, but Collingwood's views obscure the irrecoverability of the past.

Altogether, the discipline of history operates as an intrusion in the problem of entering into an understanding of living faith. Certainly, historical study of the Bible is an important path to understanding historical material in the Bible. But the discipline of history is incapable of appraising either the content or the nature of faith.

## 4.7  The Role of "Events" in Divine Revelation

Whilst the discipline of history may be no more than a spectator of the biblical witness, a claim may still be made that in some sense God has used events to disclose what he is like. If one accepts that in the Bible there is, at the least, the record of the impression of some sort of divine revelation, then the historical circumstances are integral as context to the revelation. Divorced from their biblical context, propositions about God can become abstract. When they recalled the Exodus, the Jews remembered the escape from Egypt, not the revelation of the divine name (Exodus 3:14). The Bible primarily describes what God has done rather than who he is. The demonstration of the divine character is needed as the context and as the qualifier of doctrine. Doctrine taken on its own does not appear to be an independent trait in the biblical witness. The traditions mediate both the occasion of revelation and the content of revelation.

The attempt to distil doctrine from the biblical record can cause immense problems. Particularly, if doctrine is separated from its context in tradition, a conflict can emerge which may be summarized in the response to the question: "How can an unchanging and eternal God act in a temporal world?" If doctrine is subtracted from its historical context, an immense strain is placed on the historical material that remains, because just as the doctrine has been removed from its context, so the historical narratives have suffered the loss of their content. The strain on the historical material produces a desire to substantiate its truth, or, at any rate, to safeguard it against being discredited. Hence has issued the labor of theologians to assert the compatibility of, if not integrate, theology and the discipline of history.

The established solution to the apparent tension between theology and history has been for theologians to insist on God's revelation through history. Barr has challenged this whole procedure.[23] Barr has pointed out that theologians have been unable to find a uniform validation for this approach in the Bible, and they lack any unity in their understanding of history. Furthermore, there are substantial areas of the Bible which offer no basis for any teaching of "revelation through history", for example, the book of Proverbs. Barr affirms that the main function of "revelation through history" has been apologetic. "Revelation through history" meets the thought of an age dominated by history and historical method, and shows that these are also concerns of Christianity.

However, "revelation through history" is not an adequate way of relating to the past. It is an unsound method to attempt to comprehend the Christian faith by differentiating doctrine from its context, so as to determine the content of revelation, and then reintegrate doctrine and historical material so as to give an account of what may be accepted as having been revealed through history. The illusion of security, and even certainty, about the divine revelation through history rests only on intellectual foundations, whereas remembrance incorporates doctrine and revelatory events within a richness of tradition, of which the believer is a part.

## 4.8 Progress rejected as a theology of history

Another way of relating to the past has been explored in theology and has hinged around the use of the concept of "progress". The limitations of progress and any other teleology have already been demonstrated. But the Christian vision of an improved world has had a great effect on world history. However, a theology of history which involves "progress" implies that it has been possible to resolve the theistic ambiguity of the world process so that there is a discernible revelation through history. Daniélou has attempted to build a theology of progress in history. Many of his presuppositions are embodied in his first paragraph:

> The Bible is a record of the evidence for certain
> events, certain historical works of God: such as,
> the covenant with Abraham, the birth and resur-
> rection of Jesus Christ, and Pentecost. Conse-
> quently the Christian outlook is primarily deter-
> mined by a series of divine operations, tracing a
> distinct line of development: each of these
> events marks a new stage in the actualisation of
> God's design, and a mutation of human life. Two
> aspects of the whole process are of especial im-
> portance: first the nature of the event itself, and
> of the divine decision transforming reality; and
> secondly the succession of events, exhibiting at

> once a certain continuity and a certain discontin-
> uity, i.e., by definition, progress.[24]

To describe the Bible as a record of evidence is to give a distinctly partial view of its charcter. The Bible is primarily a deposit of traditions.
But calling the Bible a record of evidence gives Daniélou the freedom to
mold the evidence to suit his own purposes. Next, he regards the salvific events as being in a line of development. Certainly, one thing happened after another, but "development" is a highly interpretative word
which implies some sort of immaturity in the earlier stages of the series. This may be an appropriate model in the understanding of the formulation of Christian doctrine, but it does not seem to fit the Biblical
understanding of the salvific sequence (cf Genesis 1:31). But Daniélou's
last point is highly contentious. He describes the succession of events
as exhibiting both continuity and discontinuity and calls this "progress". This continuity and discontinuity is the normal character of the
historical process. There is no reason why process should be identified
as progress. Optimism is not a substitute for prolegomena.

Daniélou also finds a different view of history from the perspective of
eschatology:

> The idea of an end . . . is of capital importance
> in the system, from three distinct points of view.
> First, history is not conceived as an indefinite
> progress, but as finite in scope . . . Secondly,
> Christianity is itself the term of development:
> Christ professedly comes "late in time", and in-
> augurates the stage that will not pass away. So
> there is nothing beyond Christianity . . . Third-
> ly, the end of history has already taken place,
> because the incarnation and the ascension of
> Christ fulfil its purpose.[25]

Daniélou feels that the Christian outlook on history locates the center
of interest at neither the beginning nor at the end but in the middle.
This use of the notion of progress is a highly ingenious way of focuss-
ing attention on the salvific works of Jesus Christ:

> . . . Christ's resurrection being the decisive event

> in all history, nothing that can ever happen will
> equal it in importance . . . No progress now can
> ever bring about for us what we have already got
> in Christ; that which is beyond all progress is
> here and now in him; the last stage exists already
> in the Christian mysteries.[26]

Whilst Daniélou's position may be fairly attractive from some points of view, it does not really do justice to the passage of time. Locating the focus of history in the work of Christ distracts attention from the problem of the elapse of time, and the schema fails. Daniélou's optimism again comes through in his estimation of civilization: "The Creator and the Redeemer are one and the same God. Civilization is not the devil's work: society and culture belong to creation, they are part of the work of God's hands."[27] However, civilization is as theistically ambiguous as the creation - really one can only say that "it exists", not that "it is divine". One could link to this problem an anxiety for the redemption of civilization in all its various forms - monarchy, institutions, etc. But, like Dodd's views, Daniélou's theology of progress fails on insufficiently clarified categories, and an inability to cope with the pastness of the past.

## 4.9 Divine Action as History

By contrast, Senarclens arrived at a very different estimation of history. Senarclens found the only true history in divine action. For Senarclens, Jesus Christ is the totality of truth, but historical truth is merely the subjective opinion of any particular historian. So Senarclens identified the truth of history as Jesus Christ in his death and resurrection, his judgment and his pardon, his presence and his word. Senarclens embraced divine action as solely being genuinely historical, and relegated all other history to a subordinate status. Thus he felt that the divine action in Jesus Christ gives meaning to the context in which it has taken place. This approach may be acceptable in theological polemic, but such a stance evades the normal understanding of the historical process. Normally, context gives meaning to historical content.

Barth had his own stance in this matter. For him the Biblical writings are the witness that God speaks, but it is only the present event of God's speaking that is revelation. Barth was quite definite that identifying revelation and the Bible should not be automatically assumed. Instead Barth insisted that revelation: "takes place as an event, when and where John's finger points not in vain but really pointedly, when and where by means of its word we also succeed in seeing and hearing what he saw and heard. Therefore, where the Word of God is an event, revelation and the Bible are one . . . ."[28] Whilst there maybe great reassurance in understanding effective proclamation as divine action, it is not satisfactory to assert that divine action suppresses the passage of time. The experience of a vivid re-presentation of the words of scripture is not achieved at the expense of the sequence of time, though it may still be perfectly correct to feel that one has experienced divine action.

## 4.10 The Challenge of the Temporal Remoteness of the First Century AD

It has been demonstrated that "remembrance" is a pattern of life which Christian believers are exhorted to follow in the Eucharist. There does not appear to be any bridge between the salvific events of biblical times and the present except the witness of scripture and the confessed Lordship of Jesus Christ within the continuing community of the faithful. The Lord's Supper is a "reminder to remember" and therefore to obey. The anxiety which is felt about the temporal remoteness of the life of Jesus of Nazareth cannot be legitimately dispelled by any theory which seeks to set aside the passage of time, though a severe critique of historical methodology does preclude the erosion of biblical narratives.

The many ways that have been outlined of encountering the past in the present fail because they try to avoid the passage of time. In denying the passage of time these theories can require considerable credulity and an implied distortion of the created order. Furthermore, these theories by which a believer can somehow enter into the past in the present can turn the challenge to believe into problematic exercises in the literary appreciation of the sacraments. Alternative suggestions of the dominant significance of divine action in history, or the doctrinal solutions linking past and present through the second or third Persons of the Trinity are also unacceptable.

Augustine's views about the theistic ambiguity of the world process, and the consequential impossibility of meaning or progress in history have a compelling force. There do not appear to be any grounds in the philosophy of history for gainsaying this understanding. To the spectator, the world process may or may not indicate that there is a God at work revealing himself. Consequently, the world process may or may not have a meaning or a purpose, and may or may not be going in a particular direction. With this clarification of the nature of the past there is no longer any need to look for the unambiguous divine disclosure in known history or the present. If history were without ambiguity, then faith would be a far lesser thing. This is not to deny that all things are within the Providence of God, but to affirm that he does not choose to disclose his hand. However, Augustine thought that it was possible to be confident about the meaning of biblical events as they had some sort of divine guarantee in the disclosure of their meaning.

The practice of the discipline of history requires an absence of any bias. There has to be a freedom for historians to arrive at the interpretation of their sources. If known history were not theistically ambiguous, then the art of history would have to operate within totally different parameters.

One of the by-products of the theological reliance on history has been the re-inforcement of the tendency in the Christian faith to understand revelation in terms of propositions. An imagined grounding of the tenets of faith in "historical fact" has overlooked the impossibility of historical certitude. Equally, the distress occasioned when the historical basis of the Christian faith has been challenged (eg. some of the reaction to the publication of the *Myth of God Incarnate* ) has overlooked the fact that the discipline of history is in large measure inapplicable to biblical traditions, and therefore no great dismay should be felt at the partial disengagement of history and theology. Indeed, unless these two disciplines are disengaged, the intermediate ground between them cannot be inspected.

It is worth being cautious over the use of history in theology. The writing of history yields historical writing, but has no power to authenticate religious perception. Indeed, history cannot be normative for biblical study since substantial parts of the Bible are not even cast as historical narratives. A preoccupation with establishing the historical credentials of the Christian faith may have been counter-productive, for as there is no objectivity of fact in history, history cannot support a religious conviction. Biblical traditions can be shared and participated in, but the temporal remoteness of Biblical times does not need to be evaded. The apprehension of Christian tradition should issue in a knowledge of God in which truth is relational rather than subjective/objective. This apprehension of Christian tradition is the essence of remembrance, and gives experiential content to the Lordship of Jesus Christ over History.

## 4.11 Implications for sacramental theology

In this study, a different path has been followed from that by which sacramental theology is normally examined. The standard doctrines of the eucharist (Real Presence, sacrifice, etc.) are normally only criticized in the light of each other, and the philosophical problem of the relationship of the present to the past tends to be side-stepped. This study has exposed some possible difficulties in maintaining theories of the representation of the death of Jesus Christ in the Eucharistic offering. Indeed, a wider reference is demanded than the death of the Messiah. The anamnesis clause requires that the elements be received in remembrance of Jesus Christ. While it may be desirable to decide to isolate the death of Jesus as a specific focus of remembrance, it may be a mistake for this focusing to become exclusive. If the eucharist is felt to relate to the death of Jesus Christ, then the wider context is neglected. Now when St Paul wrote (1 Corinthians 11:26): "For as often as ye eat this bread, and drink the cup, ye proclaim the Lord's death till he come", he did not, in modern scholarly consensus, mean by "proclaim" that the Corinthians represented the Lord's death symbolically with the broken bread and poured-out wine. Rather, "proclaim" here means "announce by word of mouth". So, at the common meal they recited aloud the narrative of the Passion. And there is the implication that already at the time that Paul was writing, the perspective of the remembrance of the passion had broadened to include the second coming. So the way in which in the Judaic tradition a specific focus of remembrance accrued a wider spectrum of reference continued to operate. In due course the anaphoras of the Church included the creation, incarnation, resurrection and parousia. The Eucharist of the Church having taken the place of all the Jewish feasts, the context of the season of the year varies the relative emphasis of the shades of the spectrum of remembrance within the awareness of those who share in the Church's worship.

If in the liturgy there is no evasion of the sequence of time, no bringing into the present things of the remote past, no contrivance of historical illusion, then doctrinally, this simply means that whilst those who join in anamnesis in the eucharist do so of their own volition, they have no control over any mechanism that may bring about an effective anamnesis. Torrance's view is that at the Eucharist Jesus Christ himself confers his real presence upon it, so that the anamnesis becomes effective by divine gift.[29]

## 4.12  Conclusion – Anamnesis and Discipleship

The question has to be faced as to how to harmonize the theology of remembrance with the austerity of the philosophy of history. Faith implies some view as to the meaning of tradition of the past and involvement in those traditions. The philosophy of history denies the ultimate meaning of any particular event, or collection of events.

This study has endeavored to meet this problem by noting the limitations of the discipline of history. But it has also been maintained that biblical traditions are not susceptible to the direct scrutiny of the discipline of history. This is the significance of the distinction that has arisen between "known history" and "unknown history." Scepticism is appropriate to "known history" and to the methodology of history, but scepticism is quite inappropriate to "unknown history" as mediated by tradition. Known history is represented primarily by historical evidence that has been left behind in the present. Unknown history is represented by custom, oral tradition, written tradition, and patterns of understanding. Known history relies on amalgam of awareness, understanding and discipleship. Traditions that have emerged from the past may be used to express a present faith.

One significant strand of understanding that has emerged is the Christian view of the world affairs as primarily a theatre made up of individual people. The locus of remembrance is initially, therefore, the life of the individual. Accordingly, it may be suggested that the believer is exhorted by the anamnesis clause to participate in the Eucharist as a declaration of general obedience. Obedience in this matter links in with obedience in the whole pattern of discipleship. Neither believers nor doctrine can deny the ever-widening gap of time between the time of Pontius Pilate and the present. But remembrance for the disciple is a confession of faith and a pattern of life. The Lordship of Jesus Christ over history may not be traced in the affairs of the nations, but can be declared in and through the lives of the faithful.

## NOTES

1. Popper, **The Open Society and its Enemies,** (London, 1949), Vol. II, 258.
2. McIntire, **God, History & Historians,** (New York, 1977), 56-58.
3. Dodd, **History and the Gospel,** (London, 1938), 166.
4. Ibid., 26.
5. Ibid., 26.
6. Ibid., 167-168.
7. Ibid., 28.
8. Ibid., 163-164.
9. Ibid., 164.
10. Cullmann, **Salvation in History,** (London, 1967), 315.
11. Ibid., 316.
12. Ibid., 316.
13. Ibid., 317.
14. Cullmann and Leenhardt, **Essays on the Lord's Supper,** (London, 1958), 61.
15. Dodd, **History and the Gospel,** (London, 1938), 163.
16. M. Green, **Runaway World,** (London, Inter-Varsity Press, 1969), 12.
17. Harvey, **The Historian and the Believer,** (London, 1967), 128.
18. Mascall, **Theology and History,** (London, 1962), 6.
19. Ibid., 7.
20. A. M. Ramsey, **Jesus and the Living Past,** (Oxford, 1980), 19.
21. Ibid., 8.
22. Collingwood, **The Idea of History,** (New York, 1956), 218.

23. Barr, *"Revelation through History in the Old Testament and in Modern Theology"*, in **New Theology**, No. 1, (New York, 1967), 60-74.

24. Daniélou, **The Lord of History**, (London, 1958), 1.

25. Ibid., 7.

26. Ibid., 7.

27. Ibid., 14.

28. Barth, **Church Dogmatics**, Vol. I, Pt I, (Edinburgh, Clark, 1960) 127.

29. T. F. Torrance, **Theology in Reconciliation**, (London, Chapman, 1975), 119.

# CHAPTER FIVE

# Implications for the Relationship between Church and Society: Prolegomena to Mission

## 5.1 Introduction

The unravelling that has taken place of the way that Christian believers relate to the past is important. Remembrance through the use of tradition is a major facet of the identity of the Church. The implications of all this must be pursued. The Christian practice of remembrance marks off the Church from Society, and colors their relationships. To the detached observer, the Church can appear to be preoccupied with the past, particularly with the events of the Gospel narratives, and the outsider is not party to the Church's use of the past. Therefore the Church appears to be immersed in anachronism. To base evangelism on an appeal to the historicity of the Gospel "events" may be to misrepresent the Church's use of tradition, as well as confirm the worst suspicions of those to whom the Church's mission is addressed. All these factors must be explored.

## 5.2 The believing community delineated by remembrance

### a. The contribution of the Old Testament

Many factors in the Old Testament impinge on the relationship between the Church and what may be termed "society." However, there is a considerable problem of methodology because modern studies have emphasized the complexity of the Old Testament corpus. The Old Testament is crucial for the understanding of the nature of the Church because the Old Testament is the hallmark of the context from which the New Testament proclamation emerged. The Old Testament was determinative for Jewish self-understanding as well as for Jewish sectarian self-understanding. Thus the Samaritans and the Dead Sea Community both appropriated the scriptures to their own vision of themselves. The Christian groups also appropriated the Old Testament scriptures and, in so doing, acceded in some measure to Jewish self-understanding.

Because of the complexity of the Old Testament, and the complexity of the history of Old Testament interpretation, it is impractical to treat the Old Testament writings as providing a clear analysis of the problems involved in studying the relationship between "Church" and "Society". This uncertainty is underlined by the way in which the early Christians appear themselves to have used scripture. However, in the Old Testament there is a variety of types or pictures of the self-understanding of the identity of the people of God. To make some broad generalizations: on the Exodus, the children of Israel and the people of God tended to be co-extensive; in the days of the prophets, the people of God tended to be those who had kept faith as opposed to those who had fallen from faith; in the days of the restoration after exile the people of God tended to be given an ethnic identity as against Samaritans and Gentiles. Clearly these three types are exceedingly general descriptions, but of the three, the Church adopted the prophetic model in which Christians were ministers of the true faith.

It may be affirmed that the faith of the people of Israel emerged in a world where no action was devoid of cultic implication and connotation. The reputation for legalism of the Hebrew mentality reflects an age-long effort both to secure a pattern of life which only offered allegiance to the God of Israel, and also to secure the interpretation of that pattern of life. Psalm 119.1 offers the reflection "Blessed are they that are perfect in the way, who walk in the law of the Lord", which illustrates the way that the Jews were exhorted to a distinctive and unambiguous lifestyle. Another way in which Israel was summoned to be the people of God was the exhortation to "wisdom". Ackroyd understands wisdom as "part of that mechanism by which life is to be rightly ordered."[1] Accordingly, in Deuteronomy 4.6 Israel is told concerning the statutes and judgments given them: "Keep therefore and do them; for this is your wisdom and your understanding in the sight of the peoples." Thus the people of Israel were encouraged to secure an obedience to God that should permeate their life-style, and be a sign of their distinctiveness to other nations. This was remembrance–a dedicated pattern of life that was a confession of faith. It was as a people who lived in remembrance that God is God that the Jews were delineated by their traditions.

The life of Israel was constituted as a testimony to the dominion of God. The life of Israel was dependent upon God, not upon man. The "Life of Israel" is the meaning of Israel; and the meaning of Israel is God: God reaching out to man; God striving; a people striving with God.

In view of the richness of this heritage, it is not surprising that there are no large-scale well-developed models of the Church's understanding of itself in the New Testament. It could have been expected that there would have been a major thematic illustration, using something drawn from the Old Testament, that would have been eloquent of the Church's self-understanding. But, instead, small scale pictures arise as the writers need. Thus the leaven in the lump, and even the Church as the body of Christ, are evocative, but they are not definitive. This may plausibly be suggested to be because the practice of remembrance inherited from Judaism required a complete dedication to God and his Christ rather than a narrow commitment to some pattern of self-understanding. Some people may feel that the Church has been struggling with the resultant identity crisis ever since, but the Church is committed to proclaiming the dominion of God, not the importance of the Church.

b. The implications of the New Testament for the Identity of the Church

The New Testament is the deposit of the post-resurrection Church. It is impossible to reconstruct the outline of the post resurrection Christian community, if only because this was not the intent of the written material that survived. The New Testament writings have the collective function of explaining the nature of Christianity and giving the shapes of the distinctive identity of Christianity. The distinctive identity of Christianity is indissolubly linked to the unique identity of Jesus Christ. But it is impossible to analyze the gospel material so as to determine the identity of Jesus Christ. For example, even the use of such categories as "original" and "secondary" can be self-defeating because just as nothing is certainly original, so nothing is certainly secondary. Consequently, just as it is impossible to give a clear description of the earliest Church, so it is impossible to describe its founder.

The New Testament writings are in the same way the product of the faith of the Church. Therefore, "the church's acknowledgement that just these writings are sufficient as her 'canon' is part of her self-description."[2] But because it is impossible to delineate the formal outline of the early Church, it is impossible to posit a relationship between "Church" and "Society" on the basis of a distinct and identifiable Church in the New Testament.

It may be supposed that the identity of the Church in the New Testament may be found by examining the use of the word *ekklesia*. Many scholars have affirmed that the source of the name *ekklesia* for the Christian community is the Septuagint, where the word is used to render the usual term for Israel as the people of God. So, in calling themselves the *ekklesia* the early Christians were claiming to be successors of ancient Israel and true people of God. But a more likely explanation is that the word *ekklesia* is used in the New Testament consciously to distinguish the Church from the Synagogue, for in the LXX *ekklesia* and *sunagoge* mean much the same and many times correspond to the same Hebrew word. But "the Synagogue" had come to mean primarily the local building where the Jewish congregation met, and the "Diaspora" had become the inclusive term for Jews outside the Holy Land. So the word *ekklesia* was available as a generic inclusive term for all Christians together–locally and universally. The lexical history of *ekklesia* cannot delineate the description of the Church,

There was both continuity and discontinuity between Judaism and the post-resurrection Church. This continuity and discontinuity are focussed in the recorded teaching of Jesus, and in the way that his person was understood. Jesus himself is recorded to have said: "Think not that I came to destroy the law or the prophets: I came not to destroy, but to fulfil" (Matthew 5:17). Jesus did not elaborate how he considered this fulfilment to take place, but the Church was familiar with the idea that acknowledging Jesus involved re-focussing one's understanding of the scriptures on the person of Jesus; "And beginning from Moses and from all the prophets, he interpreted to them in all the scriptures the things concerning himself" (Luke 24:27). Thus, the Church acquired an exegesis and a doctrine that were adequate to differentiate the Christian community from Judaism. For example, "resurrection" as a point of doctrine was not commonly held in an agreed formulation in Judaism and was largely absent from the teaching of Jesus. But the Church emerged as the resurrection community, and its self-awareness as such differentiated it from Judaism sufficiently for the Church not to be assimilated to the spectrum of outlook represented in Judaism. After the first Easter there emerged in Christianity a confident and articulate faith in which "resurrection" had moved from the periphery to the center.

The great development of remembrance in Judaism had safeguarded Jewish identity, but had also produced a consciously ethnic exclusivism which the new Christian communities did not wish to emulate. The Christian communities delineated their membership on the basis of confession, for example, 1 John 4:2: "every spirit which confesseth that Jesus Christ is come in the flesh is of God . . . "; or Romans 10:9: "if thou shalt confess with thy mouth Jesus as Lord, and shalt believe in thy heart that God raised him from the dead, thou shalt be saved". The problem of Christian identity that arises from the New Testament is not one of how to secure a new exclusivism, but how faith is to be distinguished in the present. Unless it is possible to distinguish the body of the faithful, it appears to be utterly impractical to begin to talk about the relationship between "Church" and "Society". As has already been spelt out, remembrance embraces the whole of life so that every part of the believer's life is a statement of dedication. Within the Christian community, this process of remembrance has its inspiration in the Eucharist—"Do this in remembrance of me" may be interpreted as "live in remembrance of my life", or "live like me", or even "let my life live in you." The Christian community, therefore, has its identity located in remembrance. Even if the Eucharist is the distinctive Christian act of worship, still it cannot be the guarantee of Christian identity. Jesus Christ indicated that people had to be assessed on their results: ". . . by their fruits ye shall know them. Not every one that saith unto me, Lord, Lord, shall enter into the kingdom of heaven, but he that doeth the will of my Father which is in heaven" (Matthew 7:20,21). Even if the Eucharist is the occasion when Christians have their attention focussed on their Lord, participation in the sacraments is still not an adequate seal of Christian identity. But Christian identity could be suggested to be expressed in a life that is sacramental.

The New Testament implies a Christian community that is marked out by traditions that are made up primarily of scripture and worship, of exegesis and doctrine. But these in themselves are not an exhaustive description of Christianity, rather they are components of remembrance. It may be objected that "remembrance" is too vague or unspecific to be the descriptive mark of the Christian community, but in the Judaeo-Christian heritage remembrance is the lifeblood of a living faith. Remembrance is not too small a thing to admit of precise description, rather it can be inferred from the New Testament that remembrance is too large and flexible an aspect of the Christian faith to be defined. This inference does not solve the problem of Christian identity, but does give direction to the efforts to resolve this problem.

## 5.3  The Value of the Discipline of History

In the introduction to this study, a call was made for an account of the way that believers relate to the past. It was suggested that such an account would explore the intermediate ground between the methodology of historical study and the philosophy of historical meaning. The results revealed a very substantial area of concern sandwiched between these twin thrusts of the discipline of history. The inapplicability of historical methodology to tradition does not of course mean that historical research has no contribution to make to the believer's involvement in traditional material. On the contrary, historical research illuminates the context of tradition, and therefore illuminates the content of tradition. Furthermore, careful historical study is a safeguard against the inappropriate use of tradition and against the allegorical extravagance that often characterized the pre-critical age of Biblical interpretation.

The review of the philosophy of historical meaning may have been felt to produce practically negative results in affirming that there is no meaning to history. But this affirmation is a useful caveat against the believer allowing the depth of meaning that may be found in the community of tradition to spill over into the secular world. This is not to preclude prophetic comment on the affairs of the world, but is to distinguish between the value of sacred tradition and secularity. The consequence of this understanding is the realization that it is impossible to develop an apologetic for Christianity within the framework of a general historical understanding.

History deals with the endless transience of life. Hence, if we seek to locate Christianity within a general historical understanding, then we bind Christianity within the transient world. But the Heavenly City will not be bound within the earthly city, even if it is on earth that the character of the Heavenly is discerned. Clearly, the independence of Christianity from the endless flux of history is to be found in its living tradition.

The teaching of Augustine has been noted as the Church's recognition of its dissociation from the secular world – to the extent that whilst the secular world provides an important part of the context for the community of tradition, the secular world is neither part of the content of tradition, nor party to the process of remembrance.

## 5.4 The Secular and the Sacred evaluation of the Past in the formation of Christian identity

The secular use of history is distinctively creative and vigorous. There is an enormous search for explanation and understanding. Historians investigate the past bringing to bear a highly trained and often sensitive inquisitiveness. The fascination of the past brings its own enchantment, and within the context of the "humanities," the discipline of history contributes to the self-understanding of mankind.

Another way in which the discipline of history contributes to the modern world is that historical study illuminates the understanding of the present. Many people feel that they can understand the present in terms of how the present came about. An investigation of the causes of the present world order leads people to investigate the past. The past has set the parameters of the present. The institutions of the present, the available modes of thought, and even the vocabulary of language are all inherited from the past.

Part of the subject matter of historical investigation is, of course, the church. Ecclesiastical history is an immense field, but the study of

church history cannot lead to a clear definition of the distinction between "church" and "society." Church history is rather a record of the
endless intermingling of "church" and "society". Consequently, it may
be noted that any formal attempt to differentiate between "church" and
"society" as separate categories should not be imposed on the life of the
Church, unless it is wished to establish a sectarian insularity. In any
case, if Christian identity is characterized by remembrance, that is too
large a thing to be incorporated in a definition.

Ecclesiastical history may teach us how the present day church came to
have its shape and patterns of denomination. But ecclesiastical history
cannot give an adequate reason for the existence of the Church. Christian believers tend to feel that their membership of the Church is tied
up with their present encounter with God. Looked at from the outside,
the observer can see only  the Church's uses of traditions. But one of
the features of the Church's uses of traditions is that traditions concerning the past are used to articulate a present experience of God.

Christian worship is dominated by traditional material. Consequently,
Chrisitian worship can be misunderstood to be a deliberate exercise in
anachronism. But tradition is not only used to focus on the past, tradition is also used to express what is felt in the present. It is in the
sphere of doctrine and doctrinal propositions that the past is focused
upon. But a good example of the spelling out of the use of tradition in
worship is the following. The tradition in this case is the tradition of
the Nativity, and the instance in which its use is articulated is the last
verse of the carol: "O little town of Bethlehem." For many years, mil-
lions of people have been singing:

> O holy child of Bethlehem,
> Descend to us, we pray;
> Cast out our sin, and enter in,
> Be born in us today.
> We hear the Christmas angels
> The great glad tidings tell:
> O come to us, abide with us,
> Our Lord Emmanuel.

Many more examples could be given from the Church's hymnody. Perhaps such examples as "When I survey the wondrous cross," "Jesus Christ is risen today," and "Come down, O Love divine" will suffice.

The distinctive Christian use of tradition, with its historical camouflage, has confused many enquirers into the dynamics of faith. It appears that enquirers have been misled by this phenomenon into imagining that some sort of telescoping of time takes place within the awareness of participators in the Judaeo-Christian cultus. A proper appreciation of the role of tradition in worship puts into relief some of the extraordinary things that have been written on this matter.

Remembrance, therefore, is not a devotional exercise in which time is warped, rather it is the case that remembrance characterizes Christian identity. Remembrance cannot be mechanical -- not merely because then discipleship could enjoy an untroubled insincerity, but also because then it would be possible to define a Christian community. Part of the problem of trying to define the "Church" is that one ends up describing a way of life rather than a corporate body with a definite membership qualification.

Remembrance appears to operate in the following way – a pattern of responsive obedience is developed issuing in a present encounter with God; and God is described through his activity. The training in remembrance may be presented as follows. The physical signs of the covenant –fringes, phylacteries, door-post symbols, and circumcision–were obligations under commandment that required responsive obedience evidently intended to cultivate an awareness of God. The Sabbath and the Passover were further obligations under commandment that demanded obedience in response and that channelled people's response towards a sense of encounter with God. These festivals encouraged people to describe God in terms of his saving activity and gave them a sense of involvement in his design. This outline is repeated again and again in the Old Testament. Thus the Lord calls Abram (Genesis 12:1), Abram responds and leaves Haran (12:4), and God is then described as the Lord who brought Abram out of Ur of the Chaldees (15:7). God commissions Moses (Exodus 3:10), Moses responds and leaves for Egypt (4:20), the Israelites leave Egypt after the plague (12:37) and God is then described as the Lord who brought the Israelites out of Egypt (13:3). Psalm 78, particularly, contains an extensive description of God in terms of his activity. The picture of God that is built up in the Old Testament through describing his activity is qualified in the New Testament by the activity of God through Jesus Christ. Once again, a pattern of responsive obedience issues in a present knowledge of God; and God is described through his activity. For example in John 1:12,13 those who receive the Word are given the right to become children of God, and then it is claimed that believers are "begotten" (RV margin) of God. However, a further stage is added to the outline of the operation of remembrance, because in the New Testament the life of the believer becomes part of the activity of God. So in Peter's speech in Acts 2, Jesus of Nazareth is described as a channel for the activity of God (v 22), and then the disciples present themselves as extensions of the activity of God through the Holy Spirit (v 33). Even Gentiles could be caught up into the activity of God (Acts 10.45). And from that stems the problem of the Church's mission--how to involve people in the activity of God when they stand outside the community of tradition. This was, of course, the problem the apostles faced as they branched out into the Greek world. In effect they had to distil a slimmed-down body of tradition that would be adequate to give context to the content of the gospel message. Obviously it was not enough merely to recite facts. As has already been noted bald facts are meaningless; facts have to be given significance. A suffering Messiah was enough to puzzle the Jews, but to the Gentiles it was a baffling message (1 Corinthians 1:23).

The pattern of remembrance that has already been outlined may well summarize the unprecedented process of the mission to the Gentiles whereby non-Jews entered into a Jewish inheritance: responsive obedience issues in a present encounter with God; God is recognized as the one who brought about the obedience; the life of the believer becomes part of the activity of God.

Assuming that it is possible to define the Church as a gathered community one could profitably explore the character of the Church as consisting of those engaged in the process of remembrance. Responsive obedience appears to be the gateway to the community of tradition.

The "past" takes on different roles in different contexts. In tradition, the past is used to express the content of the present. The hymn "Guide me, O thou great Jehovah", for example, uses the metaphors of the exodus wanderings, the crossing of the Jordan, and the settlement in the promised land, to deal with the pilgrimage of faith and going through and beyond the experience of death. The problem then, of course, arises as to whether such a use of the past is a manipulation of the past so as to deprive the past of its true meaning. At a time when there has been concern about the credibility of the Gospel and the biblical narratives, it might have been thought wiser to refrain from this way of using biblical motifs. But it is surely reasonable to use the metaphors of the past as being analogically appropriate to the present experience of believers.

However, it is one thing to sample the hymnody and even the canticles and psalmody of the twentieth century Christian community, it is quite another thing to apply these insights to the prayer of consecration at the Holy Communion.

## 5.5 Remembrance in the Eucharistic Prayers

At the center of the institution narrative lie two simple commands: "Take, eat," and "Drink this." Clearly, these afford a simple, straightforward opportunity for responsive obedience. But the response is not left in a vacuum, and is given direction by the anamnesis clause: "do this in remembrance of me". The communicant is reminded to remember the reality of Jesus Christ. The designation of the bread and wine as the body and blood of the Son of God is evidently not the only focus of the institution narrative, but further serves as a declaration of the corporal reality of Jesus Christ–thereby disclaiming docetism and other doctrinal aberrations. The images of the breaking of the body and the shedding of the blood do not limit the communicant to the remembrance of the crucifixion, but also serve to underline the reality of Jesus Christ and his commitment to the divine plan.

The description of the body and blood as that "which was given for you" and that "which was shed for you" declare the saving purposes of God through Jesus Christ and the communicant acknowledges that activity of God in the reception of the elements. The act of reception may not be a passive acceptance of the elements, so much as the communicant's active recognition of the saving activity of God through Jesus Christ. D. M. Baillie, in a passage of almost celestial prose, expressed this insight as follows: ". . . while in the sacrament it is profoundly true that God is the giver and we are the receivers, it is also true that receiving God means giving ourselves to Him; and indeed . . . God's giving of Himself to us and our giving of ourselves to Him are but two ways of describing the same thing."[3]

The context that is given to the institution narratives shades the recognition of the activity of God into involvement in the activity of God through Jesus Christ. The reality that is affirmed of Jesus Christ in the institution narrative becomes identified, through context and through the physical sign of participation in the new covenant, with the reality of the believer. Consequently, the brokenness in sacrifice of the acknowledged Lord becomes exhortatively exemplary and the anamnesis clause becomes effectively an injunction to "Do as I have done." In this way the believer has the opportunity to become an extension of the activity of God.

All this is not to set aside patterns of devotion revolving around the Real Presence, but is an attempt to explore how the institution narrative functions from the perspective of an analysis based on an appreciation of the significance of anamnesis in the Judaeo-Christian tradition. Perhaps such a perspective affords insight into the inspirational power of the eucharist. Clearly, if anamnesis is a pattern of life rather than a detail of devotion, the eucharist becomes of fundamental relevance to discipleship.

## 5.6 Living Tradition

At this point it may be felt that a rather unsatisfactory juncture has been reached. The demands of remembrance have turned the Church and the eucharist into rather fluid entities. But it may be affirmed that this fluidity is desirable rather than regrettable. A clearly defined church may in itself be a barrier to mission because the yardstick for commitment is the hurdle of a definition rather than an individual's response to the opportunities for his individuality. Equally the eucharist that is straitjacketed may have little exhortative appeal, and be devoid of challenge or encouragement to the communicant.

This is not an evasion of intellectual rigor, but an appreciation of the impossibility of applying clear-cut categories to living tradition. Tradition lives through the process of remembrance. Bare recital is merely repetition of tradition. But tradition comes alive by people entering into it. The role of tradition in a living community of believers is not susceptible to easy analysis, particularly when remembrance directs the allegiance of believers beyond the community. To treat such an intangible web of motivations and relationships is impossible if the vibrancy of the living reality of the Church has to be reduced to a formal model. But the advantage of a description of the process of remembrance in the community, and in its central act of corporate worship, lies in that the dynamism of the community is reflected rather than excluded as it can be in a structured analysis. Consequently, the study of anamnesis has an important contribution to make to ecclesiology.

Furthermore, the study of anamnesis has a significant contribution to make to the theology of mission. There does not seem to have been any examination of the way individuals are incorporated into the believing community through entering into the process of remembrance. Assent to doctrinal formulae may be desirable but cannot be equated with incorporation into a living tradition. Of course doctrine is essential to the Church's self-understanding, but doctrine can never present an exhaustive description of the life of the Church. Assent to the Church's self-understanding, and assent to the credal formations of the Church is not the same as incorporation into the Church. Indeed, it could be suggested that the historical tenets of the faith tend to receive assent because of their felt analogical appropriateness to the life of the believer.

Baptism is the mark of Christian initiation. But initiation has to be complemented by incorporation. It was evinced above that this process of incorporation is fulfilled in the life of the believer becoming part of the activity of God. This fulfillment has often been expressed in terms of the Holy Spirit coming into the life of the believer. The analysis afforded by the approach of anamnesis does not discount the biblical, doctrinal and experiential significance of the Holy Spirit. Indeed, an appreciation of remembrance is of assistance in understanding the channels through which the divine enters human experience. But the study of anamnesis also has a valuable contribution to make because this aspect of the religious experience of the believer affirms the integrity of the believer. We have noted earlier the way in which the eucharist affirms the reality of Jesus Christ, and the way in which his reality becomes identified with the reality of the believer. Now, it has often been felt that one of the problems of an unqualified doctrine of the Holy Spirit is that it may lead to what has been termed "Pneumatological Docetism". This tendency arises from attributing such a plenary act of indwelling of the Holy Spirit that the humanity of believers is superseded if not abolished. The study of anamnesis, in affirming the integrity of believers, and the involvement of their humanity in the process of remembrance, acts as an important control on any extravagant pneumatology.

The process of remembrance gives context to the indwelling Spirit. A believer may apprehend the Holy Spirit within his or her person. Such apprehensions are inevitably self-authenticating and do not necessarily entail a moral connotation. Thus the miracle of healing does not automatically lead to a moral life for the one healed. Similarly, glossolalia is no guard against moral collapse. But any doctrine of the Holy Spirit which speaks of the Spirit within the individual should be morally significant for the person who is indwelt.

The implications for the doctrine of the Holy Spirit of a study of the process of remembrance for the life of the indwelt believer and community are practical and ethical. Just as the believer cannot properly contain the effects of sanctification within himself or herself, so also the community of tradition cannot be introverted, but discloses its inner life through its outward activity.

## 5.7 Conclusion – The Community of Tradition in Dialogue with the World

It may be felt to be ponderous to refer to the Church as the "community of tradition". But it is desirable to use this terminology in this study both to emphasize the function of the Church and also to underline its distinctiveness. "Church" means many things in many different denominations. The local churches in centers of population are not homogeneous and there are usually many differences between neighboring churches even of the same denomination. These differences may reflect the subtle influences of different personalities, but different personalities tend to yield different theological emphases. Furthermore, given the frequent autonomy of local congregations, let alone cathedral chapters, it may be deduced that the formal organization of the churches encourages local diversity. And it is only proper that there should be local diversity, if the church is in any way to respond to the localities in which it is established.

But whatever the denomination, and wherever two or three believers are gathered together, those who meet are caught up in a process of remembrance and encounter (cf. Matthew 18:20). Clearly the Church does not live to itself–rather it lives for God to the world. If a congregation fails to look beyond itself, then the process of remembrance is stifled. The central act of worship of the majority of denominations has at its center the anamnesis clause, with its implication "Live as I have lived". If a congregation is inward-looking rather than outward-looking, it is impossible to live as Jesus Christ lived. Mission is essential to the Church. If a community of tradition does not go out in responsive obedience, then the force of the tradition is either misapplied or denied.

It has been shown that outreach is necessary to the dynamism of the community of tradition. This final chapter has set out to explore the implications of the study of anamnesis for the relationship between church and society, particularly with regard to drawing out some prolegomena to mission. Naturally it is reasonable to assume that if a community of tradition is engaged in a process of remembrance it should have a high estimation of the value of its internal life. Furthermore, it is also natural that if the community has a high estimate of its internal life it should seek to incorporate others in its shared life and in an encounter with God.

This chapter has shown that the church can be described qualitatively as the community of tradition, and the internal process of remembrance is demonstrated in behavior and mission. It may be affirmed that only by the Church being the Church in this way can it express and safeguard its identity. It has not been possible to adduce any other way of securing the identity of the Church. It may be noted that only by the believers in a community of tradition making their convictions vulnerable through behavior and mission can the identity of the community be secured.

This study had its origin in the quest to discover the significance of the anamnesis clause. The extent of the spectrum of subjects that have been touched upon in this pursuit is a testimony to the central importance of the eucharist in the worship of the Church. The conclusions of this study are positive and present the life of the Church as a dynamic force in the world.

## NOTES

1. Ackroyd, **Exile and Restoration**, (London, 1972), 255.
2. Kelsey, **The Uses of Scripture in Recent Theology**, (London, 1975), 106.
3. D. M. Baillie, **The Theology of the Sacraments**, (London, 1957), 115.

# BIBLIOGRAPHY

Ackroyd, P. R. *Exile and Restoration*. London: SCM, 1972.

Augustine, *The City of God*, Edited by D. Knowles: Harmondsworth, Middlesex: Penguin, 1980.

Baillie, D. M. T*he Theology of the Sacraments*. London: Faber, 1957.

Baillie, J. *The Belief in Progress*. London: Oxford University Press, 1951.

Barr, J. *Biblical Words for Time*. London: SCM, 1969.

Barr, J. "Revelation through History in the Old Testament and in Modern Theology" in *New Theology*, No. 1, edited by M. E. Marty and D.G. Peerman, New York: Macmillan, 1967: 60-74.

Berkhof, H. *Christ the Meaning of History*. London: SCM, 1966.

Berlin, I. *Historical Inevitability*. London: Oxford University Press, 1955.

Bradley, F. H. "The Presuppositions of Critical History" in *Collected Essays*. Vol. I. Oxford: Clarendon Press, 1935.

Brandon, S. G. F. *Time and Mankind*. London: Hutchinson, 1951.

Bultmann, R. *History and Eschatology*. (The Gifford Lectures, 1955), Edinburgh: University Press, 1957.

Bultmann, R. *Jesus Christ and Mythology*, New York: Scribner, 1958.

Burgelin, P. *L'Homme et le Temps*. Paris: Aubier, 1945.

Butterfield, H. *Christianity and History*. London: Bell, 1950.

Carr, E. H. *What is History?* Harmondsworth, Middlesex: Penguin, 1973.

Carnley, P. *The Structure of Resurrection Belief*. Oxford: Clarendon Press, 1987.

Childs, B. S. *Memory and Tradition in Israel*. London: SCM Press, 1962.

Clements, R. *God's Chosen People*. London: SCM, 1968.

Collingwood, R. G. *The Idea of History*. New York: Oxford University Press, 1956.

Cullmann, O. *Christ and Time*. London: SCM, 1957.

----- *Salvation in History*. London: SCM, 1967.

----- and Leenhardt, J. *Essays on the Lord's Supper*. London: Lutterworth, 1958.

Dahl, N. A. "Anamnesis: Memoire et Commémoration dans le Christianisme Primitif" in *Studia Theologica*, Vol. I, 1947.

Daly, R. J. *The Origins of the Christian Doctrine of Sacrifice*. London: Darton, Longman & Todd, 1978.

Daniélou, J. *The Lord of History*. London: Longmans, 1958.

Danto, A. C. *Analytical Philosophy of History*. London: Cambridge University Press, 1968.

Dawson, C. *The Dynamics of World History*. London: Sheed and Ward, 1957.

Dentan, R. C. *The Knowledge of God in Ancient Israel*. New York: Seabury Press, 1968.

De Vries, S. J. *Yesterday, Today and Tomorrow - Time and History in the Old Testament*. London: SPCK, 1975.

Dix, G. *Jew and Greek*. London: Dacre Press, 1953.

Dodd, C. H. *History and the Gospel*. London: Nisbet, 1938.

----- *The Authority of the Bible*. London: Nisbet, 1944.

Downing, F. G. *The Church and Jesus*. London: SCM, 1968.

Dyson, A. O. *The Immortality of the Past*. London: SCM, 1974.

Ehrenberg, V. *State and Deity*. London: Methuen, 1974.

Eichrodt, W. *Theology of the Old Testament*. Vol. I, London: SCM, 1975.

Evans, C. F. *Resurrection and the New Testament*. London:

Fackenheim, E. L. *Metaphysics and Historicity*. Milwaukee: Marquette University Press, 1961.

Friedlander, M. *The Jewish Religion*. London: Shapiro, Vallentine, 1953.

Gardiner, P. "Historical Understanding and the Empiricist Tradition" in *British Analytical Philosophy*. Edited by B. Williams and A. Montefiore. London: Routledge & Kegan Paul, 1966.

Gellner, E. *Thought and Change*. London: Weidenfeld & Nicholson, 1969.

Ginsberg, M. *The Idea of Progress*. London: Methuen, 1953.

Gore, C. *The Body of Christ*. London: Murray, 1901.

Goudzwaard, B. *Capitalism and Progress*. Toronto: Wedge, 1979.

Gregg, D. *Anamnesis in the Eucharist*. Bramcote, Notts: Grove Books, 1976.

Gregor Smith, R. *Secular Christianity*. London: Collins, 1966.

Gunneweg, A. H. J. *Understanding the Old Testament*. London: SCM, 1978.

Hanson, R. P. C. *Eucharistic Offering in the Early Church*. Bramcote, Notts: Grove Books, 1979.

Harris, N. *Beliefs in Society*. London: Watts, 1968.

Harvey, V. A. *The Historian and the Believer*. London: SCM, 1968.

Hayek, F. A. *Law, Legislation and Liberty*. Vol. I. London: Routledge and Kegan Paul, 1973.

Hengel, M. *The Atonement*. London: SCM, 1981.

Holy Bible. Revised version. London: BFBS, 1965.

Huizinga, J. "The Idea of History" in *The Varieties of History*. Edited by F. Stern. London: Macmillan, 1970.

Jasper, R. C. D., and G. J. Cumming, editors, *Prayers of the Eucharist: Early and Reformed*. London: Collins, 1975.

Jaubert, A. *La Date de la Cène*. Paris: Lecoffre, 1957.

Jeremias, J. *The Eucharistic Words of Jesus*. Oxford: Blackwell 1955.

Johnston, G. *The Doctrine of the Church in the New Testament*. Cambridge: Cambridge University Press, 1943.

Jones, C., et al., editors, *The Study of Liturgy*. London: SPCK, 1978.

Jones, D. "Anamnesis in the LXX and the Interpretation of I Cor. XI v 25" in *Journal of Theological Studies*, Vol. VI. Oxford: Clarendon Press, 1955.

Kelsey, D. H. *The Uses of Scripture in Recent Theology*. London: SCM, 1975.

Kilpatrick, G. D. "Anamnesis" in *Liturgical Review*. May, 1975.

Knight, D. A., editor, *Tradition and Theology in the Old Testament*. London: SPCK, 1977.

Ladd, G. E. *The Presence of the Future*. London, SPCK, 1980.

Lewis, H. D. *Freedom and History*. London: Allen & Unwin, 1962.

Lewis, M. M. *Language in Society*. London: Nelson, 1947.

Löwith, K. *Meaning in History*. Chicago: University of Chicago Press, 1967.

----- *Nature, History and Existentialism*. Evanston: Northwestern University Press, 1966.

McIntire, C. T., editor, *God, History and Historians*. New York: Oxford University Press, 1977.

Markus, R. A. *Saeculum: History and Society in the Theology of St. Augustine.* Cambridge:   University Press, 1970.

Martin-Achard, R. *A Light to the Nations.* Edinburgh, 1962.

Marrou, H. I. *The Meaning of History.* Dublin:   Helicon, 1966.

-----*Time and Timeliness.* New York:   Sheed & Ward, 1969.

Marsden, G. and F. Roberts, editors, *A Christian View of History?* Grand Rapids: Eerdmans, 1975.

Marwick, A. *The Nature of History.* London:   Macmillan, 1973.

Mascall, E. L. *Theology and History.* London:   Faith Press, 1962.

Minear, P. S. *Images of the Church in the New Testament.* London: Lutterworth, 1961.

Momigliano, A. "Time in Ancient Historiography" in *History and the Concept of Time--Beiheft 6 of History and Theory.* Middletown, Connecticut:   Wesleyan University Press, 1966.

Moran, G. *Theology of Revelation.* London:   Search Press, 1973.


Nations, A. L. "Historical Criticism and the Current Methodological Crisis" in *Scottish Journal of Theology,* Vol. 36, No. 1, 1983.

Nicol, I. "History and Transcendence" in *God, Secularisation and History.* edited by E. T. Long. Columbia, South Carolina: University of South Carolina Press, 1974.

North, C. R. *The Old Testament Interpretation of History.* London:   Epworth Press, 1953.


Oakeley, H. D. *History and the Self.* London: Williams & Norgate, 1934.

----- "The Status of the Past" in *Proceedings of the Aristotelian Society,* Vol. XXXII. London:   Harrison, 1932.

Oakeshott, M. *On History and other Essays.* Oxford:   Blackwell, 1983.

Ogletree, T. W. *Christian Faith and History--A Critical Comparison of Ernst Troeltsch and Karl Barth.* New York: Abingdon Press, 1965.


Patrides, C. A. *The Phoenix and the Ladder:  The Rise and Decline of the Christian View of History.* Berkeley: University of California Press, 1974.

Plantinga, T. *Historical Understanding in the Thought of Wilhelm Dilthey.* Toronto:   University of Toronto Press, 1980.

Polak, F. *The Image of the Future.* Amsterdam:   Elsevier Scientific Publishing Co., 1973.

Popper, K. R. *The Open Society and its Enemies.* London: Routledge & Kegan Paul, 1949.

-----*The Poverty of Historicism.* London:   Routledge & Kegan Paul, 1961.


Preiss, T. "The Vision of History in the New Testament" in *On the Mean ing of History--Papers of the Ecumenical Institute* No. V,Geneva: Oikumene, 1950: 48-66.

Ramsey, A. M. *Jesus and the Living Past*. Oxford: Oxford University Press, 1980.

Richardson, A. *History, Sacred and Profane*. London: SCM Press, 1964.

-----*An Introduction to the Theology of the New Testament*. London: SCM, 1958.

Richardson, P. *Israel in the Apostolic Church*. Cambridge: Cambridge University Press, 1969.

Rickman, H. P., editor, *Meaning in History. W. Dilthey's Thoughts on History and Society*. London: Allen & Unwin, 1961.

Riesenfeld, H. *Jésus Transfiguré*. Copenhagen: Munksgaard, 1947.

Robinson, J. M. and J. B. Cobb, editors, "New Frontiers in Theology," Vol. 3: *Theology as History*. New York: Harper & Row, 1967.

Rowley, H. H. *The Biblical Doctrine of Election*. London: Lutterworth, 1950.


Saunders, R. M. "Voltaire's View of the Meaning of History" in *University of Toronto Quarterly*, Vol. 22, 1952.

Schnackenburg, R. *The Church in the New Testament*. London: Burns & Oates, 1965.

Schopenhauer, A. *The World as Will and Representation*. Vol. II, New York: Dover, 1966.

Schutz, A. *The Phenomenology of the Social World*. London: Heinemann, 1980.

Senarclens, J. de, *Le Mystère de L'Histoire*. (Doctoral Thesis in the University of Geneva), Geneva: Roulet, 1949.

Sklair, L. *The Sociology of Progress*. London: Routledge & Kegan Paul, 1970.

Smart, J. D. *The Interpretation of Scripture*. London: SCM, 1961.

Spiegel, S. *The Last Trial*. New York: Behrman House Inc., 1979.


Thurian, M. *L'Eucharistie*. Paris: Delachaux, 1959.

Torrance, T. F. *Theology in Reconciliation*. London: Chapman, 1975.


Vaux, R. de., *Ancient Israel: Its Life and Institutions*. London: Darton, Longman & Todd, 1974.

Vermes, G. *Scripture and Tradition in Judaism*. Leiden: Brill, 1973.

von Rad, G., *Old Testament Theology*, Vol. I. London: SCM, 1975.

Vos, W. and G. Wainwright, editors. *Liturgical Time*. Rotterdam: Liturgical Ecumenical Center Trust, 1982.

Walsh, W. H. "Colligatory Concepts in History" in *The Philosophy of History* edited by P. Gardiner. London: Oxford University Press, 1974.

-----"Meaning in History" in *Theories of History* edited by P. Gardiner, New York: Free Press, 1966.

-----*Introduction to the Philosophy of History*. London: Hutchinson, 1967.

Zimmerli, W. *The Old Testament and the World*. London: SPCK, 1976.

**DATE DUE**

| MAR 1 5 '90 | | | |
|---|---|---|---|
| 4/24/17 | | | |
| | | | |
| | | | |
| | | | |
| | | | |
| | | | |
| | | | |
| | | | |
| | | | |
| | | | |
| | | | |
| | | | |
| | | | |
| | | | |

HIGHSMITH    # 45220